06114

Maidenhead Library
St Ives Road
Tel: 01628 796969

KT-148-081

Please return/renew this item by the last
date shown. Books may also be renewed
by phone or Internet.

www.rbwm.gov.uk/web/libraries.htm

01628 796969 (library hours)

0303 123 0035 (24 hours)

The Royal Borough
Windsor &
Maidenhead

Windsor and Maidenhead

38067100590792

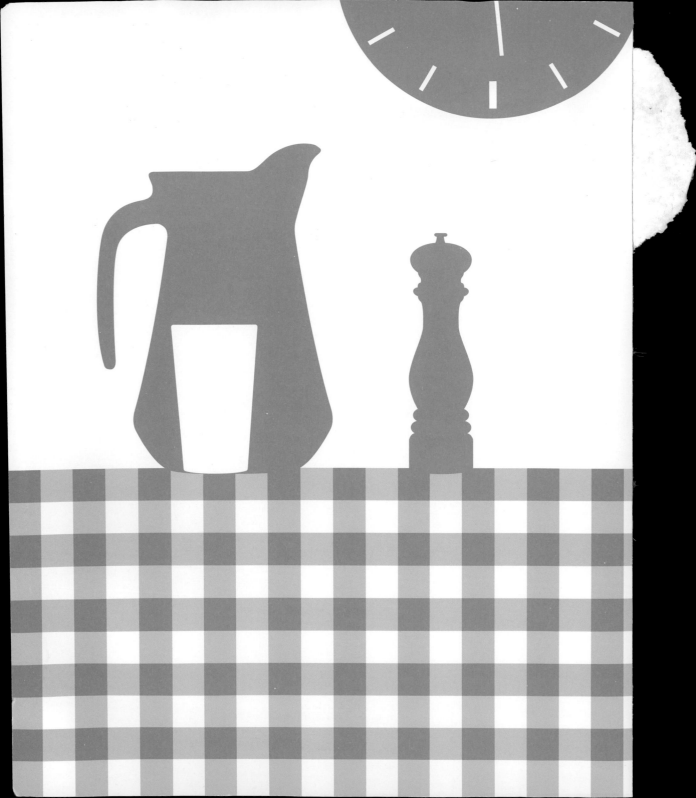

The After School Cookbook

NICK COFFER

HODDER &
STOUGHTON

First published in Great Britain in 2014 by
Hodder & Stoughton
An Hachette UK company

1

Copyright © Nick Coffer 2014

The right of Nick Coffer to be identified as the Author of the Work
has been asserted by him in accordance with the Copyright,
Designs and Patents Act 1988.

All rights reserved. No part of this publication may be
reproduced, stored in a retrieval system, or transmitted, in any
form or by any means without the prior written permission of
the publisher, nor be otherwise circulated in any form of binding
or cover other than that in which it is published and without a
similar condition being imposed on the subsequent purchaser.

A CIP catalogue record for this title is available from the
British Library

Trade Paperback ISBN 978 1 444 71373 2
Ebook ISBN 978 1 444 78327 8

Designed by Bobby Birchall, Bobby&Co
Typeset in Glypha LT Std

Printed and bound in China by C&C Offset Printing Co. Ltd.

Hodder & Stoughton policy is to use papers that are natural,
renewable and recyclable products and made from wood grown
in sustainable forests. The logging and manufacturing processes
are expected to conform to the environmental regulations of the
country of origin.

Hodder & Stoughton Ltd
338 Euston Road
London NW1 3BH

www.hodder.co.uk

Contents

Introduction

With a six-year-old son at school and a three-year-old daughter growing up too quickly, the need for after-school food inspiration is acute in our house. And, if what I hear from fellow parents is anything to go by, our house is certainly not unique.

That's why I actually need this book! And I am confident that you do too.

Schoolchildren of any age need nutritious and tasty food, fast. They need energy food. They need food to keep them going before they go to football or Brownies or music practice. They need lunch boxes with fun things in them to make a change from jam sandwiches. They need parents who can cope with a group of school friends coming home for unplanned and chaotic play dates.

And as for us parents, we need time. But we don't have any of that. So we need food that will save us time. Food that is hassle-free. Food that fits into an ever-tighter family budget. Food our children will actually eat and which we can just as happily enjoy ourselves, either with our children or later in the evening when they are in bed asleep.*

* In our house, being in bed and actually being asleep are not necessarily concurrent activities.

Our children would love us to consistently produce marvellous treats in an eye blink. But with our own busy schedules to contend with, we need to find meals to keep everyone happy that we can cook around all of our timetables. And, most importantly, we need to juggle all of this to get food on the table at the *right* time because their tired heads can't cope with waiting.

There have been times when I have felt that reconciling all of the above was actually impossible. Especially when you throw children's unpredictable food tastes into the mix: when a curry can be a hero on a Tuesday and a pantomime villain on a Wednesday.

And all that is why I have written this book.

In the **Speed of Night** chapter you will find dishes that can be on the table literally minutes after you walk through the door. There are meals you can stretch over two days in two different forms in **Here Today, Still Here Tomorrow. Inspired Lunchboxes** goes well beyond soggy sandwiches (and all of the recipes here will act as great lunches or light meals in their own right too) and there are loads of fantastically frugal ideas in **Saving your Bacon**. I have also picked out some of the most popular supermarket ready-meals and turned them into **Ready-Made Meals, Made by You**. Crispy pancakes, chicken Kievs and a cheat's lasagne are among many home-made treats to beat the ping-and-ding of microwave meals with limited effort. There's also a brilliant chapter of food which can be prepared in advance with minimum fuss so it can be **Ready When You Get Home** and, not forgetting the fun, there is a raft of wonderful **Genius Treats** to round off any meal in style.

2+2=7 turns mealtimes into the main event when you have a full house. This chapter is packed with low-effort meals for unexpected play dates. Sociable, fun and guaranteed to impress your discerning young guests, all of these recipes have been stress-tested during the most stressful of after-school shenanigans.

And, by popular demand in my house, I have addressed the ever-pressing issue of The Gap. The Gap is when your child comes out of school, hungry and in need of instant refuelling but it's too early for supper and they quite possibly have somewhere to shoot off to before they will be able to eat a full meal. Maybe they are heading to an activity or you are planning to do some shopping with them in tow. The chapter entitled **Mind the Gap** deals with that need perfectly.

As with everything I cook, the food in this book is not simplified 'kids' food'. This is food for adults to love too. And if you plonk a coriander leaf on top or serve it in a posh bowl, nearly all of the food here wouldn't look out of place at a dinner party among friends either.

All the signature elements of my first book are still here. This is a book chock-full of great family recipes, for everyone to cook together and eat together. Equally, all of the recipes can be served early for the children and eaten later by their parents when the house is a little calmer.

And, as before, techniques are always simple, recipes are forgiving and foolproof and ALL the ingredients are widely available. In fact, I'd even go as far as to say that all but a very small handful of the ingredients are available from the smaller local versions of the big supermarkets. This is important for me as lack of time (and planning) often means I stop off on the way home from work to grab some simple ingredients to throw together for an emergency supper.

So, while the nature of my recipes has not changed in the three years since I published my first book, much else has. Archie is at school, I'm no longer a stay-at-home dad, as I've started a new career, Matilda has joined the family, and my wife is a busy psychotherapist.

Which takes me back to what I said at beginning: **I need this book!**

Cooking with children

As I have always said, once you accept the inevitable mess, cooking with your children is one of the most fun things you can do together. That's why what I really do miss are the almost daily cooking mash-ups I used to enjoy with Archie when he was little and not yet at school and I was a stay-at-home dad. As I have documented so many times before, this was always precious quality time for both of us, and a wonderful learning experience to boot. It's no exaggeration to say that his hours in the kitchen have led to him being a proper little cook.

It's not that we don't cook together any more. We just do it less, which in some ways makes it all the more fun and precious when we do. If Archie isn't too tired after his school day, he loves creating havoc with me in the kitchen. In truth though, weekends are now the preferred time for cooking together. The funniest part is that his sister is following exactly the same path as he did. Everyone knows how children try to emulate their elder siblings and the time spent in our kitchen is a prime example of that. It's rather lovely really, as Archie adopts a gentle helping-hand approach with his firebrand little sister, showing the kind of patience I always tried to show him when he was a toddler. It has also been interesting to see that it wasn't just a one-off with Archie; when children help in the kitchen there is more chance of them eating what they have prepared.

I've not made suggestions for what steps your children can help with, as it really depends on how confident they are in the kitchen and what they've done before. I'd suggest very young children stick to mixing and stirring, and then progress to simple chopping with a normal dining knife when they're a bit older. It goes without saying that only older children should be in charge of hot saucepans and the oven, and always with your eyes on them at all times!

New ingredients, new equipment

As my family kitchen has evolved, so has my cooking and the equipment I use for it. A slow cooker is a wonderfully affordable addition to any busy family home. And, at the other end of the speed scale, my pressure cooker enables me to make dishes in barely 20 or 30 minutes that would take 2 or 3 hours if cooked conventionally. The rather cumbersome (and slightly unsafe) pressure cookers I remember my mum using 30 years ago are now long gone and forty quid will see you buying a good model which will last an age. Both these cookers are investments you won't regret making, not least because they both love turning cheap cuts of meat into meltingly flavoursome meals. For that alone, they pay for themselves in time. I have got back into fondues recently too, and as such have included three fondue recipes in the 2+2=7 chapter (although two of them can be made without an actual fondue kit). Ours was just a cheap version and, again, it has more than paid for itself in the number of times it has been used.

There is nothing in this book that cannot be made from ingredients that are easily to hand. You may want to make sure your spice cupboard is well stocked, and some good wine vinegars and cider vinegars will come in handy, as will a block of creamed coconut. And with beans so good for you – and so cheap too – they are used a lot in this book, so a few spare tins on the shelves will stand you in good stead. The same goes for lentils. Basically, as long as you have a good range of staples in your kitchen, you'll be able to make fantastic meals every night of the week.

As you will find as you cook the recipes in this book, nothing will fall apart if you are missing an ingredient or two. Feel free to leave out what you don't have – and to add in what you do. This book is all about flexible recipes, which will forgive on even the most stressful of evenings.

Vegetarian recipes and special dietary requirements

I'm conscious of the growing interest in meat-free cooking, and so over half of the recipes in this book are vegetarian or can be easily adapted to be meat-free.

VEGETARIAN

I've also considered the growing need for gluten-free and dairy-free diets and so there are lots of recipes here that are suitable for anyone following these diets. There are also some specifically gluten-free desserts in the Genius Treats chapter.

Preparation, cooking times and portions

All the recipes in this book have been tested by me and by a wonderfully generous group of mums and dads who offered to try out the recipes to make sure they are popular with adults and children alike when served at the dinner table.

I want everyone to enjoy these recipes, no matter how experienced you are in the kitchen, so I have rated them: 'very very easy', 'very easy' or 'easy'. Every recipe is wholly manageable even for a moderately confident cook.

VERY VERY EASY

VERY EASY

EASY

The time each recipe takes is ranked as 'really really quick', 'really quick' or 'quick'. With the focus on simplicity, no recipe in the book merits long preparation.

REALLY REALLY QUICK

REALLY QUICK

QUICK

You'll also notice that some recipes are labelled 'slow'. These are perfect for when you want to put a meal on to cook and forget about it while you get on with something else.

SLOW

You can share your thoughts about the recipes in this book on twitter: @nickcoffer, facebook/MyDaddyCooks, and my blog: MyDaddyCooks.com.
Happy cooking!

Nick

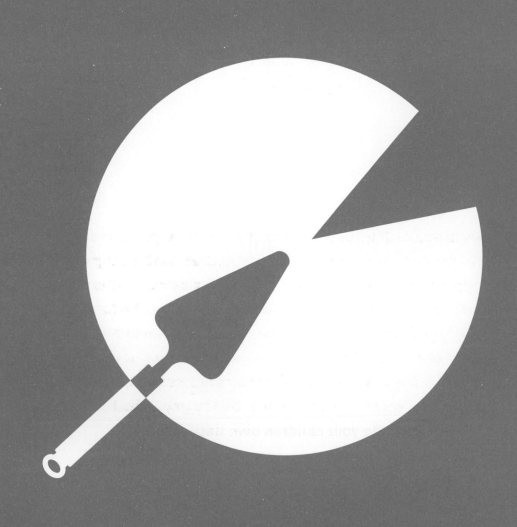

Mind
the Gap

When you pick up your children from school, you may still be a couple of hours away from suppertime. And during that gap they may be going off to football practice, Guides or Scouts, they may have a music lesson, or you may be (bravely) about to drag them around the shops. This is where this chapter comes into its own. These recipes are not quite meals (although some come close) but they are mostly much more than snacks. Guaranteed to fill the gap, refuel and tide your children over until supper.

Italian eggy bread croque-monsieur

You are going to have to cut me a bit of slack here! I just couldn't think of the right title so, I figured, if in doubt, just tell it like it is. So this is indeed an Italianesque sandwich, which really is halfway between a croque-monsieur and eggy bread (as we always call it in our house). Most importantly, this is a filling and frankly delicious after-school snack. If you are not serving it immediately, wrap it in some aluminium foil and it will keep while you take it on the school run.

Makes 2 sandwiches

1 tablespoon tomato purée

A small handful of fresh basil, chopped

1 small garlic clove, crushed

4 slices of bread

1 ball of mozzarella cheese, sliced

4 thin slices of ham

Salt and freshly ground black pepper

1 large egg, beaten

4 tablespoons milk

Olive oil

Butter

1. Mix together the purée with basil and garlic. Spread it over 2 of the slices of bread.
2. Layer over the mozzarella and the ham, leaving a border of around 2cm (to prevent the cheese dripping out when frying). Season with salt and pepper.
3. Top each sandwich with another slice of bread and squash together firmly.
4. Mix the eggs and milk in a shallow bowl, dip the sandwiches into the mixture and coat well.
5. Heat a dash of olive oil and a large knob of butter in a wide frying pan on a medium heat. Fry the sandwiches on each side until golden brown.
6. Serve immediately or wrap in foil for later.

Cheddar, Parma ham and courgette scones

Break time, lunchtime or, in this case, at the school gates, these light and flavoursome scones are almost a meal in their own right. If Archie wolfs down three of these, he is happily full for the rest of the evening. And why not? Meat, veg and dairy, all in a very simple and light traditional scone. As with the fritters on page 155, making scones is a great way of using up whatever cold meats and vegetables you may have in your fridge that are reaching the point of no return.

Preheat your oven to 220°C/425°F/Gas Mark 7.

1. Mix the flour and paprika with a little salt and pepper in a bowl. Add the butter and rub it in using the tips of your fingers until it looks like a crumble mix.
2. Give the grated courgette a good squeeze to remove any excess water, and then stir it into the crumb mix with the cheese and ham.
3. Mix the eggs and buttermilk together in a bowl. Make a well in the flour mix and pour in the wet mixture. Stir it lightly with your hands to combine and form a dough.
4. Turn out the dough onto a floured surface and knead it lightly until smooth (you won't get a perfectly smooth dough, thanks to the added courgette, cheese and ham).
5. Roll out the dough to a thickness of around 3cm and cut into rounds, preferably using a scone cutter but you can really use any roundish cutter shape you have (I like to use the rim of a tall tumbler).
6. Place the scones on a non-stick baking tray. Brush with the beaten egg and sprinkle with cheese.
7. Bake in the oven for 20 to 25 minutes until the scones have risen and are golden brown.
8. These scones can be eaten warm or they can keep for a maximum of a day in an airtight container (they will dry out a little overnight though).

Makes about 12 scones

450g self-raising flour, plus extra for dusting

½ teaspoon paprika

Salt and freshly ground black pepper

175g butter, broken into small lumps

1 smallish courgette, grated

100g grated extra-mature Cheddar cheese

50g Parma ham, chopped (or regular ham)

2 eggs

6 tablespoons buttermilk

For the topping

1 egg, beaten

Freshly grated Parmesan or Cheddar cheese, for sprinkling

Tuna and tomato empanadillas

Life is definitely too short to make your own puff pastry so a store-bought block is at the heart of these empanadillas. Capers are funny things, really. Individually, they have such a strong flavour and yet they work so well with tuna and tomatoes. The capers and olives will likely be more than salty enough so there is no need to season the filling with salt. If you prefer, instead of baking the empanadillas, you can fry them for a couple of minutes either side in oil on a medium heat, which will save you a little time.

Makes 8–10

2 tablespoons olive oil

1 small onion, finely chopped

3 ripe tomatoes, finely chopped

185g tin tuna (preferably in oil or spring water), drained

1 tablespoon green olives, finely chopped

1 tablespoon capers, rinsed and chopped

Freshly ground black pepper

1 hard-boiled egg, chopped

Flour, for dusting

500g packet of puff pastry

1 egg, beaten

Preheat the oven to 200°C/400°F/Gas Mark 6.

1. Heat the olive oil in a frying pan over a medium heat and cook the onion for 4 to 5 minutes until soft. Add the tomatoes and cook until reduced and only very slightly wet.

2. Remove the pan from the heat and stir in the tuna, olives and capers. Season with pepper and then very gently stir in the hard-boiled egg. You want the filling to be quite dry so that it doesn't make the pastry wet.

3. On a floured worktop, roll out the puff pastry to a thickness of 3–5mm and cut out as many 15cm rounds as you can (I use a small plate or saucer as a template). You should get 8 to 10.

4. Spoon a heaped tablespoon of the mixture onto each round, a little off centre. Now, wet the edge of the pastry with some of the beaten egg, fold one side over and seal gently. Crimp with a fork and brush with more beaten egg. Place the empanadillas on a non-stick baking tray.

5. Bake in the oven for 20 to 25 minutes until nicely puffed up and golden brown. Serve warm or cold.

Vegetarian scotch eggs

It goes without saying that you can turn these into classic sausage Scotch eggs by using the meat from a couple of sausages to replace the vegetable and chickpea mix, but this vegetarian version is just as, well, meaty and full of good stuff. These Scotch eggs work well as stopgap snacks because eggs themselves are filling, without being unnecessarily heavy. And, if your children are crafty types (I mean crafty as in they like doing crafts, not as in sneaky, naughty and cheeky!), they will enjoy assembling these Scotch eggs.

1. Cook the eggs in simmering water for 5 minutes exactly, then cool them down immediately in ice-cold water (or, better still, a bowl of ice). This will stop them cooking and leave the yolks a little runny.

2. Now make the filling. Heat some olive oil in a pan on a medium heat and fry the onion, carrot, beetroot and garlic for about 5 minutes until soft. Add the spices and lemon zest and stir well.

3. Crush the chickpeas using a fork or masher (you don't want them to be completely smooth) and mix them in with the other filling ingredients. Remove the pan from the heat.

4. To assemble, peel the eggs, dry them with kitchen paper and dust them in flour.

5. Divide the filling into 4 equal pieces. Dust your hands with flour and flatten each piece into a large oval about one and a half times the size of the egg (it will be roughly 3–4mm thick). Mould each piece around an egg so that the filling completely covers the egg.

6. Dip each egg in the beaten egg and then coat in breadcrumbs, making sure they're evenly and fully covered.

7. Heat a deep-fat fryer to 180°C (or a saucepan, one-third full with oil – test the temperature of the oil by dropping in a small cube of bread. If it browns and crisps up in 15 seconds, it is hot enough). Fry the eggs until golden brown – around 3 minutes. You can also shallow fry them in 5mm oil – just keep turning them so they brown evenly all over.

Makes 4

4 large eggs, plus 1 egg, beaten

Olive oil

1 onion, finely chopped

1 carrot, grated

1 small beetroot, finely grated

2 garlic cloves, crushed

1 teaspoon cumin

A pinch of ground cinnamon

Zest of 1 lemon

400g tin chickpeas, rinsed and drained

2–3 tablespoons plain flour

Fine breadcrumbs (panko breadcrumbs are excellent for this)

Vegetable oil, for deep-frying

Chicken and butternut squash pasties

Makes 6

Olive oil

Butter

1 onion, finely chopped

1 clove garlic, crushed

1–2cm cube of fresh ginger, grated

150g butternut squash, cut into small cubes

2 chicken breasts, skin removed, cut into cubes

1 teaspoon curry powder

Salt and freshly ground black pepper

A squeeze of lime juice

2 tablespoons crème fraîche

Flour, for dusting

1 x quantity of shortcrust pastry (see recipe for chard and Gruyère tart on page 42)

1 egg, beaten

To think that my conversion to butternut squash is relatively recent! Up until about five years ago, I just couldn't even consider eating it. It was one of those totally irrational food dislikes, possibly going back to soggy carrots at school when I was six. Squash is now a regular feature in our house, be it in soups, casseroles or, as is the case here, as a filling for a pie or pasty. The sweetness of the squash is a great match for the ginger and squeeze of lime juice, and the crème fraîche ensures the chicken breast stays moist. And of course, their grabbability (I think I may have made up that word) makes these the perfect mind-the-gap snack.

Preheat your oven to 190°C/375°F/Gas Mark 5.

1. Heat a good drizzle of olive oil and a small knob of butter in a frying pan on a medium heat. Throw in the onion and cook for 4 to 5 minutes until it is softened, then add the garlic, ginger, butternut squash and chicken. Keep stirring until the chicken is just cooked on the outside.
2. Sprinkle over the curry powder, season with some salt and pepper and add a splash of water. Leave this to cook for about 5 minutes – you need it to be quite dry so that it doesn't make the pastry wet.
3. Squeeze in some lime juice and stir in the crème fraîche.
4. On a floured worktop, roll out the pastry to a thickness of 4–5mm. Cut out six rounds, each about 15cm in diameter (a small plate or saucer makes a good template.)

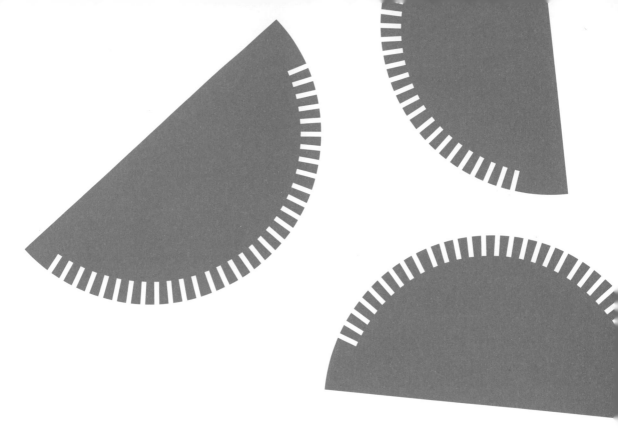

5. Divide the chicken mixture into 6 and place a portion in the middle of each round (keeping away from the edges or else the mixture will splodge out when you seal the pasties).

6. Wet the edge of the pastry with some of the beaten egg and fold one side over, pressing it together firmly. Either press around the edge with a fork or crimp with your fingers to seal.

7. Brush with more of the beaten egg, place on a baking tray and bake for 25 to 30 minutes until golden brown.

8. You can serve these fresh out of the oven or chilled.

Quick nachos with melted cheese and tomato salsa

Serves 2 children

For the salsa

4 tomatoes, deseeded and chopped

½ red onion, finely chopped

Juice of 1 lime

A pinch of sugar

½ teaspoon cumin

Salt and freshly ground black pepper

A small handful of coriander (leaves and stems), chopped

A pinch of cayenne pepper or chilli powder, to taste (optional)

A drizzle of olive oil

For the nachos

200g tortilla chips

100g grated Cheddar cheese

A small handful of chopped jalapeños (optional)

You can make a more elaborate version of this with your own guacamole, but we are talking quick, after-school gap fillers here and time is of the essence. Ideally, you would cook these in the kind of foil trays you get with takeaways and take them to school with you in the car. You can also create your own trays by using a double layer of aluminium foil. At the risk of contradicting the quick USP of this recipe, you can also make your own tortilla chips very easily using tortilla wraps cut into triangles and baked in the oven (see below). It will add an extra 10 minutes to your cooking time but, if you prefer to serve baked rather than fried crisps, this is a good option.

Preheat your oven to 220°C/425°F/Gas Mark 7.

1. Make the salsa by simply mixing together all the ingredients.
2. Divide the tortilla chips between a couple of foil trays and sprinkle with the cheese (and the jalapeños, if using). Cook in the oven for about 5 minutes until the cheese has melted.
3. Take the trays out of the oven, spoon over the salsa and either serve immediately or wrap well in foil to keep warm.
4. To make your own tortilla chips, cut 4 corn tortillas each into 6 triangles. Brush them lightly with oil, sprinkle with salt and arrange them on a couple of baking trays, making sure they aren't touching. Bake in the oven at 180°C for 8 to 10 minutes until crisp and golden.

Chewy flapjacks with seeds, coconut and dried fruit

Give your children a power boost with these flapjacks, which are brimful of good things. The beauty of flapjacks is that they are almost impossible to get wrong as they basically involve two steps: mix then bake. These flapjacks will last a good while in an airtight container and can easily be made totally vegan by replacing the butter with coconut oil and the honey with maple syrup.

Preheat your oven to 190°C/375°F/Gas Mark 5.

1. Put the butter, sugar and honey in a saucepan on a low heat. Melt them together, then simply stir in all the remaining ingredients.
2. Tip the mixture into a greased 20 x 30cm baking tray (or you can line the tray with greaseproof paper instead) and smooth it out with a knife.
3. Bake for 15 to 20 minutes until the top is nice and golden brown.
4. Allow to cool slightly before cutting into squares, then leave in the tin to cool completely. Once cool, store the flapjacks in an airtight container.

Makes 24 pieces

You will need a 30 x 20cm deep baking tray

250g butter or coconut oil, plus extra for greasing

125g soft light brown sugar

6 generous tablespoons honey or maple syrup

400g porridge oats

100g desiccated coconut

50g chopped dates

50g currants, raisins or sultanas

50g mixed seeds

Traditional Spanish omelette

The perfect quick French omelette is cooked in a searing pan and is ready on the table in a matter of minutes. Spanish omelette, however, is at totally the opposite end of the scale in terms of preparation and technique. Whereas the French one is a screechy sports car of an omelette, this Spanish omelette is a gentle meander down a breezy seafront on a warm late-summer's day. With a stop-off for beer. In less poetic terms, the Spanish omelette needs time and a little love. Still incredibly simple, it will not want to be rushed. The reward will be a truly traditional omelette, with the lovely rich, deep, sweet onion flavour that typifies the dish. The other reward I get for the TLC I put into this omelette is seeing my children almost inhale the end result. Needless to say, although this works as a mind-the-gap snack, it is just as much at home in a lunch box or as an evening meal, served with a green salad.

Makes 8 portions

250ml olive oil

1 large white onion, thinly sliced

550g waxy potatoes (e.g. Maris Piper or Desiree), peeled and cut into 3–4mm thick slices

6 large eggs, beaten in a large bowl

Salt and freshly ground black pepper

1. Heat the olive oil in a large frying pan with a lid on a medium heat. You don't want the oil to be smoking hot. Add the onions and potatoes, partially cover the pan and cook for 25 to 30 minutes. They need to cook nice and slowly, on a low simmer. There's no need to stir or mix them at this stage, but they will need an occasional nudge in the pan with a wooden spoon so they don't burn or stick to the bottom.

2. When the onions are translucent and the potatoes are soft, drain them in a colander set over a heatproof bowl and save the cooking oil.

3. Season the egg generously with salt and pepper, then mix the potatoes and onions into the bowl too. It is very important to do it this way round, rather than pouring the egg on to the cooked vegetables, so that they get a nice even coating.

4. Put the pan back on the same medium heat and pour in a really good glug of the cooking oil. Carefully add the egg mixture and give the pan a gentle shake to even out the surface. Leave it until the omelette is about 80 per cent cooked – again, no mixing or stirring. It will be coming away from the edge of the pan and still be a little liquid in the middle.

5. Place a large plate (bigger than the pan) on top of the pan (with the base of the plate facing up) and hold it tightly while flipping the pan over. The omelette will drop on to the plate. Slide it back into the pan, complete with any juices, and cook for a further 5 minutes until fully cooked through – although it should have a slight springiness when you press down on the middle.

6. Turn the omelette out on to a plate and serve warm or chilled.

Toasted gap-fillers

This is not quite as obvious as it may sound. I wanted to include some quick toasted snacks without simply saying Marmite on toast (although I do believe that Marmite on toast with Cheddar cheese is one of the greatest things ever). So, beyond the obvious, I wanted to create two lovely toppings for toast, which are very portable (meaning that they don't easily fall off), perfect for the car journey between school and Brownies or football practice. I am making these two toasted treats as open sandwiches (going the whole hog on lovely thick-cut doorstep single slices) but you can also turn them into toasted sandwiches, by lightly toasting the bread, then frying the sandwich in a pan or, of course, by simply putting it in a sandwich maker. Oh, and one more thing: you can combine these sweet and savoury suggestions: banana, peanut butter and bacon is said to have been Elvis's favourite sandwich! (Probably best to leave out the avocado from that combo though!)

The sweet
Banana and peanut butter

I enjoy omitting the sugar here and adding a spread of jam instead. Cherry or plum work particularly well.

For 2 slices of toast

Peanut butter

1 large banana, sliced very thinly

A squeeze of lime juice

A pinch of ground cinnamon

A sprinkling of brown sugar

1. Spread each slice thickly with the peanut butter.
2. Put the banana in a bowl and mix with the lime juice, cinnamon and brown sugar.
3. Mash very lightly, so it is still very chunky (you really don't want a mush). Pile on top of the nut butter and press down.

Mashed avocado with bacon and tomatoes

1. Put the chopped bacon or lardons in a frying pan with a little drizzle of oil and fry it until it browns and crisps up.
2. Add the lime juice to the mashed avocado and season with salt and pepper.
3. Stir the bacon, tomato and red onion into the avocado, adding the cayenne pepper or hot sauce if you'd like some heat.
4. Pile it all on to hot buttered toast and push down firmly.

For 2 slices of toast

2 rashers of bacon, chopped (or a handful of lardons)

Olive oil

1 tablespoon lime juice

1 avocado, mashed

Salt and freshly ground black pepper

1 tomato, deseeded and finely chopped

¼ red onion, finely chopped

A pinch of cayenne pepper or a dash of hot sauce (optional)

Lemony nut, seed and chickpea mix

This tangy, home-baked nut-and-seed mix is so moreish that I think I should market it myself! Not sure what I would call the brand though. Actually, how about 'Nutty Kids'?! This full-of-goodness snack will act as a wholesome energy boost when it is most needed. I have used citric acid, as it is fairly easily available in supermarkets, chemists and high street health food shops, but don't drive yourself mad trying to find it: lemon juice works fine, as does the North African spice, sumac.

Makes 4 servings

400g tin chickpeas, rinsed and drained

Olive oil

Salt and freshly ground black pepper

1 teaspoon of curry powder or garam masala or ½ teaspoon ground cumin and ½ teaspoon ground coriander

A pinch of ground cinnamon

½ teaspoon citric acid or 1 teaspoon lemon juice

50g nuts of any sort (almonds are perfect)

50g mixed seeds (pumpkin, sunflower and sesame all work well)

50g raisins

Preheat the oven to 200°C/400°F/Gas Mark 6.

1. Put the chickpeas on a clean tea towel, fold it over and rub gently. Some of the chickpea skins will now be stuck to the tea towel, but it's not essential to remove them all.
2. Put the chickpeas in a shallow baking dish, add a good glug of olive oil, season with salt and pepper and add the spices, including the citric acid (or lemon juice or sumac). Mix well to coat the chickpeas.
3. Cook in the oven for 20 to 30 minutes, shaking the dish every so often, until the chickpeas have dried out a little and are turning dark brown. When you think they are close to being done, stir in the nuts, seeds and raisins for a final 5 minutes.
4. Remove from the oven and leave to cool. This nut and seed mix will keep for up to a week in an airtight container.

Fruit and nut chocolate balls

This is really a three-word recipe: melt, mix, roll. Simple, failsafe, full of good stuff and, as with so many of the recipes in this book, extremely versatile. Oh, and they are pretty too! You can slip these into a school bag for a break-time snack and energy boost or just as easily pop them on a breakfast plate for a nutritious early morning treat. Just a little tip with ingredients like desiccated coconut: hunt them out in the specialist food aisles of your supermarket and you will find them at half the price of the major UK brands.

1. Melt the peanut butter and honey or maple syrup in a saucepan on a gentle heat. Remove the saucepan from the heat and stir in all the other ingredients.
2. Form into small balls in the palm of your hand, then roll the balls in the desiccated coconut and chill in the fridge.
3. These can be kept in an airtight container in the fridge for a good few days.

Makes as many as you want!

200g peanut butter

100ml honey or maple syrup

75g finely chopped nuts (almonds or cashews are especially good here)

75g dried fruit, finely chopped (I like to use a mixture of dates, apricots, raisins and blueberries)

75g mixed seeds (a combination of sunflower, pumpkin and sesame works well)

2 tablespoons cocoa powder

50g desiccated coconut, plus around 100g for rolling

Ready When You Get Home

If this book could play music, right now it would be playing some very laid-back lounge-style music while you nonchalantly pick a recipe, prepare it and cook it, in the full knowledge that it will be sitting there ready for when you get back from the school run. You certainly don't need a slow cooker to make these recipes but, if you have one, it will come into its own in this chapter. I think some of the recipes will surprise you. The pork chilli con carne is a big favourite in my house – and a lighter, cheaper alternative to beef. And my love of all things French (from living there for most of my twenties) means I couldn't resist sharing my wonderful garbure recipe with you (see page 40). Your children will love this thick, soupy casserole.

Beef stew with herbed dumplings

Serves 2 adults and 2 children

2 tablespoons plain flour

1 teaspoon freshly ground black pepper

½ teaspoon cayenne pepper or mustard powder

Salt

Olive oil (or beef dripping)

750g beef stewing steak

1kg root vegetables (try a mixture of carrots, swede, celeriac and even beetroot), cut into 3cm chunks

2 sticks of celery, thickly sliced

1 onion, thickly sliced

2 garlic cloves, chopped

1 teaspoon crushed fennel seeds or star anise

1 strip of orange zest (optional)

A bouquet garni made from sprigs of thyme and flat-leaf parsley and a bay leaf tied together (or a store-bought one)

100ml red wine or cider

1 tablespoon wholegrain mustard

400ml beef stock or water

If you want to make this stew extra-economical, seek out ox cheeks to use instead of stewing steak – they are very similar in flavour, but with a moister texture (you can probably only find them at your butcher's though). Don't for a moment think this is a spicy stew; lightly spiced is the best way to describe it. A traditional stew with a little warming edge. My notoriously spice-averse children don't view this as spicy, which is a pretty good barometer for me. The dumplings are the perfect accompaniment for mopping up the juices left on your plate.

If you want to make this in a slow cooker, simply brown everything as described below and cook in a slow cooker for 4 hours on high or 8 hours on low. Add the dumplings for the last 45 minutes.

Preheat the oven to 160°C/325°F/Gas Mark 3.

1. In a shallow bowl, mix the flour with the black pepper and cayenne pepper and some salt. Toss the steak in the flour mixture to coat it on all sides.
2. Heat a glug of olive oil (or some beef dripping for total authenticity) in a large casserole over a medium to high heat and fry the beef in batches until brown all over.
3. Remove the beef and transfer it to a plate. Add the vegetables (including the celery and onion) and garlic to the casserole and cook, stirring occasionally until they are lightly browned.
4. Stir in the fennel seeds and orange zest, if using, and add the bouquet garni, then pour over the wine or cider and allow it to bubble for a minute or so. Give everything a good stir, scraping off anything stuck to the bottom of the casserole for extra taste.

5. Add the mustard and stock and return the beef to the casserole. Put the lid on and cook in the oven for around 2 hours.

6. To make the dumplings, mix together all the ingredients and season with salt and pepper. Add water, 1 tablespoon at a time, mixing until you have a fairly sticky dough. Break this into 8 pieces and form rough dumpling shapes.

6. After the 2 hours of cooking time is up, drop the dumplings on top of the beef casserole and return it to the oven, uncovered, for a further 15 to 20 minutes until they are golden brown.

7. Serve immediately.

For the dumplings

200g self-raising flour

100g suet (vegetarian or beef)

1 teaspoon mixed dried herbs

1 teaspoon mustard powder

Salt and freshly ground black pepper

Pork chilli con carne

Serves 2 adults and 2 children

Vegetable oil

500g pork, cut into 1cm cubes

1 onion, finely chopped

3 garlic cloves, finely chopped

2 teaspoons ground cumin

2 teaspoons ground oregano

A small bunch of coriander

400g tin chopped tomatoes

1 tablespoon chipotle paste, or less to taste (any variant of chilli sauce or cayenne pepper can be used, but you won't get the lovely smoky warmth of the chipotle chillies)

400g tin beans (pinto, black or kidney beans all work here), rinsed and drained

200ml stock or water

Sour cream and grated Cheddar cheese, to serve

Using diced pork instead of minced beef makes this chilli slightly lighter and also cuts down on eating too much red meat, which is something we have been trying to do in our house. The pork also seems to perfectly complement the gentle spicing of the dish. I am a convert to chipotle paste, which is readily available in all large supermarkets and adds a smoky warmth to the chilli. Ideally you should add the paste during cooking so that the flavours can really develop in the sauce, but I tend to put just a drop in and then add some more to my own plate at the table, so as not to inflict my love of hot spice on the rest of the family! This is, of course, best served with rice but Archie simply loves flour tortillas and insists on rolling his chilli into a wrap.

1. Pour a really good glug of vegetable oil into a large casserole on a medium to high heat.
2. Throw in your diced pork and cook until it has browned nicely on all sides. Then add your chopped onion. Keep stirring the pork and the onion for about 5 minutes until the onion softens.
3. Add the garlic, cumin and oregano. Finely chop the coriander stems, reserving the leaves for the end of the cooking. Add the chopped stems to the casserole, along with the tomatoes, chipotle paste and beans. Pour in the stock or water.
4. Cover the casserole, reduce the heat and simmer gently for 45 minutes. Remove the lid and simmer for a further 15 minutes to reduce and thicken the sauce.
5. Coarsely chop the coriander leaves and chuck them in right at the end.
6. Serve with rice and top with sour cream and Cheddar.

For a vegetarian version

Replace the pork with 90g dried red lentils or 400g tinned
red lentils, rinsed and drained. Throw the dried lentils
in once the tomato sauce is made and cook the chilli
following the rest of the recipe instructions. If you're using
tinned lentils, add them for the final 15 minutes of cooking
time, while it's reducing and thickening. Keep an eye on the
sauce in case it needs a little extra water while cooking.

Chicken and mushroom cannelloni

Serves 2 adults and 2 children

You will need a 20 x 30cm baking dish

25g dried mushrooms, soaked in warm water for 15 minutes

Olive oil

Butter

100g mushrooms (preferably chestnut mushrooms), sliced

1 garlic clove, finely chopped

1 teaspoon thyme, chopped

2 chicken breasts, skin removed, cut into small pieces

Salt and freshly ground black pepper

200g ricotta cheese

50g grated hard cheese (such as Cheddar or Parmesan), plus extra to sprinkle on top

A squeeze of lemon juice

6 tubes of cannelloni (approx. 250g)

In recent years, the cost of dried mushrooms has dropped significantly and they have become a great store-cupboard staple. I always try to have a packet in my own cupboard, because with them there I know I can make a simple pasta dish in a matter of minutes (just soak them in water for a few minutes, then fry them in a little olive oil with a couple of cloves of garlic and a handful of chopped fresh flat-leaf parsley). They add a lovely hearty flavour to this cannelloni bake but, if you prefer not to use them, extra chestnut mushrooms (which have more flavour than white mushrooms) will do the trick well enough.

Preheat your oven to 190°C/375°F/Gas Mark 5.

1. Drain the dried mushrooms, reserving the liquid but making sure there is no grit left in it (grit is never going to taste nice in any dish!). Finely chop the mushrooms.
2. Heat a drizzle of olive oil and a knob of butter in a frying pan over a medium heat. Add the dried and fresh mushrooms, along with the garlic and thyme and cook for a couple of minutes, stirring.
3. Throw in the chicken and continue to stir for a few minutes until it is cooked through.
4. Season with salt and pepper and pour in the mushroom-soaking liquid. Simmer for a couple of minutes and then remove from the heat.
5. Stir in the ricotta and hard cheese. Taste, and season with a little more salt and pepper if you think it needs it. Add a squeeze of lemon juice. The filling is now ready. Set aside while you make the sauce.

6. Fry the onion and garlic in a glug of olive oil over a medium heat for 4 to 5 minutes until soft. Add the tomatoes, a pinch of sugar and 200ml water. Season with salt and pepper, then simmer until the sauce is slightly reduced. Be aware that you need the sauce to be quite wet in order to cook the cannelloni.

7. Carefully spoon the mushroom and chicken mixture into the cannelloni tubes.

8. Spread a little tomato sauce across the bottom your baking dish. Arrange the stuffed cannelloni tubes on top and pour over the rest of the sauce. The sauce should cover the surface of the cannelloni, but they won't be completely submerged. Sprinkle over some extra cheese.

9. Bake for around 30 minutes until everything is cooked through and nicely browned on top.

For the sauce

1 onion, finely chopped
2 garlic cloves, crushed
Olive oil
400g tin chopped tomatoes
A pinch of sugar
Salt and freshly ground black pepper

Prawn, sausage and bacon 'bog'

Serves 2 adults and 2 children

Olive oil

100g smoked streaky bacon or smoked gammon, cut into small cubes

6 pork sausages, sliced into rounds

1 onion, finely chopped

½ teaspoon dried oregano

250g long-grain rice, rinsed well

750ml chicken stock or water

2 ripe tomatoes, finely chopped

Juice of ½ lemon

1 teaspoon Worcester sauce

½ teaspoon cayenne pepper or paprika, to taste

100g green beans, sliced into 2cm lengths

250g shelled king prawns

Chopped flat-leaf parsley, to serve

This recipe is not dissimilar to a jambalaya and has it roots in the southern states of the USA. Think of it as a rice dish with a slightly soupy feel – hence the term 'bog'. The prawns can be viewed as an optional extra, but I love the added flavour they bring and they also mean the dish offers up a full 'surf and turf' experience! This is proper hearty, honest cooking and, bearing in mind my love of sausages and bacon, not far from my ideal supper. As an added bonus, throwing in the green beans at the end turns this into a true one-pot meal.

1. Heat a small drizzle of olive oil in a large casserole or saucepan over a medium heat. Fry the bacon until the fat starts running off and the bacon has crisped up, then transfer the bacon to a plate. Add the sausages to the pan, fry them until they are browned all over, then remove them from the pan and add them to the plate with the bacon.

2. Add the onion and oregano to the pan and fry them in the flavoured oil for 4 to 5 minutes, until the onion is soft.

3. Pour in the rice, give it a good stir and then add the chicken stock, tomatoes, lemon juice, Worcester sauce and cayenne pepper or paprika. Stir to combine everything, then season with a little salt and pepper and simmer for 20 minutes.

4. Return the bacon and sausages to the pan along with the green beans and cook for 10 minutes. Finally, the prawns go in and you want to carry on simmering until they are cooked through (they will be completely opaque and pink). The texture should be soupy, not dry. If it looks as though it might be drying out, add a little more stock or water and if it, conversely, looks just a little too wet, continue to cook it for a minute or two to get the right consistency.

5. Just before serving, taste for seasoning and add more lemon juice, Worcester sauce or cayenne pepper if necessary.

6. Serve with lots of chopped parsley sprinkled over the top.

Slow cooker Boston baked beans with bacon, pork and sausages

This recipe will definitely result in leftovers but I think it tastes even better the next day, and it freezes beautifully (defrost before reheating or cook from frozen in the microwave). With recipes like this – where making extra doesn't actually require any extra effort – it makes sense to err on the side of making a very large batch. Using a slow cooker will give you a richer, sweeter finished dish, but you can easily cook these lovely beans in a normal oven.

1. If your slow cooker has a browning function, heat a glug of olive oil in its base; otherwise, heat some oil in a frying pan on a high heat. Quickly fry the bacon, pork belly and sausages until lightly browned on all sides.

2. Put all the ingredients into your slow cooker and pour in enough water to cover by 2cm. Season with salt and pepper – you won't need much salt, as the bacon and sausages will already be quite salty. Cook for 8 hours on low or 4 hours on medium. Most of the liquid will have reduced down and the sauce should be thick and sweet. Taste and add more treacle if you think it needs it. If it looks just a little too liquid, cook for a bit longer.

3. If you are not using a slow cooker, brown the meat in some olive oil in a casserole over a medium heat. Pour in the red wine and boil it off before chucking in everything else. Cover and cook in an oven preheated to 140°C/275°F/Gas Mark 1 for about 3 hours, uncovering the casserole dish for the final 30 minutes. Add a little extra water if needed.

Serves 2 adults and 2 children

Olive oil

100g smoked bacon, cut into 2cm chunks

250g pork belly, cut into 2cm chunks

8 pork sausages

3 x 400g tins haricot beans, rinsed and drained

1 onion, studded with 2 cloves

2 bay leaves

100ml red wine

400g tin chopped tomatoes

1 tablespoon Dijon mustard

1 tablespoon black treacle

1 tablespoon brown sugar

Salt and freshly ground black pepper

Garbure

Serves 2 adults and 2 children

2 duck legs (skin on)

6 Toulouse sausages (or other strongly flavoured sausages)

½ white cabbage, sliced into wedges

2 carrots, sliced

1 small swede, cut into chunks

2 small turnips, cut into wedges

2 potatoes, cut into chunks

2 leeks, sliced into rounds

1 onion, halved and sliced

4 garlic cloves, chopped

A bouquet garni made from sprigs of thyme and flat-leaf parsley and a bay leaf tied together (or a store-bought one)

A pinch of ground cloves (optional)

1 teaspoon dried oregano

500ml chicken stock or water

2 x 400g tins cannellini beans (you can also use haricot beans), rinsed and drained

Salt and freshly ground black pepper

Chopped flat-leaf parsley, to serve

I really wanted to put a duck dish in this book. Duck legs are excellent value in most supermarkets and butchers. Also, both my children love eating duck (a habit that started, no doubt, in our local Chinese restaurant). This is a simple take on a French cassoulet-style dish. In simple terms, it's meat, beans and root veg in a flavoursome broth, and it goes a very long way. This lot will serve four people with plenty to spare.

1. Heat a large casserole on a high heat. Put the duck legs (without oil) in the hot pan and fry them until they are very well browned and have released a lot of fat. Remove the duck legs and transfer them to a plate. Quickly brown the sausages in the hot fat, and then remove them too.

2. Fry all the vegetables in the duck fat until they start to take on a little colour. You might have to do this in more than one batch, depending on the size of your pan. Add the garlic, bouquet garni, cloves, if using, and oregano. Return the duck legs and sausages to the pan and pour over the stock or water with an extra 250ml water.

3. Finally, add the beans, season well with salt and pepper, and simmer on the lowest heat for around an hour, until the vegetables are cooked through and the meat is falling away from the duck legs. Check regularly to make sure it doesn't dry out – add a splash more water if you think it needs it. You want the texture to be thick, but not dry, like a heavy soup.

4. To serve, remove the duck legs from the casserole. Leave them to cool for a few minutes then pull the meat away from the bones before stirring the chunks back through the garbure. You can also cut up the sausages.

5. This is a meal in one so all that needs to be done is to serve the garbure in bowls, sprinkled with lots of chopped parsley.

Spanish-style chicken with chickpeas and potatoes

Is there a better value ingredient than chorizo? A good-quality chorizo sausage immediately adds three things to any dish: flavour, texture and, of course, colour. That's a lot to get from one ingredient. Tomatoes and chicken are two of its favourite bedfellows, and they combine here to make a wonderful evening meal. If you prefer, you can cut back a little on the chicken by adding more chickpeas.

**Serves 2 adults and
2 children**

2 cooking chorizo sausages
(regular sausage length)
cut into rounds *

8 chicken thighs or
drumsticks, skin and bone
removed, cut in half **

4 garlic cloves, crushed

Zest of ½ lemon

1 teaspoon sweet paprika

Cayenne pepper or hot
paprika, to taste

A pinch of saffron, soaked
in water (optional)

1 bay leaf

500ml chicken stock or
water

400g tin chickpeas, rinsed
and drained

250g small new potatoes,
left whole

Salt and freshly ground
black pepper

2 tomatoes, chopped (or
a good glug of passata)

1 tablespoon sherry
(optional)

A squeeze of lemon juice

A handful of chopped
flat-leaf parsley

1. Put the chorizo in a large casserole on a medium heat and fry it until its lovely red oil is released. Add the chicken pieces, coating them in the oil, and fry until they are nicely browned (or should that be reddened?!).
2. Add the garlic and lemon zest, and sprinkle over the paprika and cayenne pepper, if using. Stir to coat, then chuck in the saffron along with the bay leaf, the chicken stock (or water), the chickpeas and the potatoes. Season with some salt and pepper.
3. Simmer for half an hour or so until the potatoes are cooked. Add the tomatoes and continue to simmer for another 30 minutes, topping up with a little water if it starts to dry out.
4. Just before serving, stir through the optional sherry and a good squeeze of lemon juice and sprinkle over the chopped parsley.

* if you can't find the semi-cured cooking chorizo, use the fully cured, hard, chorizo instead

** to remove the skin from the drumsticks, use a piece of kitchen paper for extra grip. Start at the meaty end of the drumstick and keep pulling, then give it a good tug

Gruyère and chard (or Tenderstem broccoli) tart

Makes 8 slices

You will need a 25cm
round tart tin

200g Swiss chard or broccoli,
roughly chopped

A squeeze of lemon juice

125g grated Gruyère or other
flavoursome hard cheese
(Emmental works well, as
does Cheddar)

3 eggs, beaten

200ml single cream

Salt and freshly ground black
pepper

Freshly grated nutmeg, to
taste

For the shortcrust pastry

300g roll of shortcrust pastry
OR
200g plain flour, plus extra
for dusting

Salt

50g chilled butter, broken
into small lumps

50g chilled lard, broken into
small lumps

Chard, the allotment growers' favourite, works
especially well in a tart like this. It is readily available
in most supermarkets but, if for any reason you are
struggling to find it, Tenderstem broccoli makes a
great alternative. In fact, you have carte blanche when
choosing which greens to use here. Serve with simple
boiled potatoes and some lovely sliced ripe tomatoes
and vinaigrette. Any leftovers will sneak perfectly into
a lunch box the day after. The addition of lard to the
pastry adds to the flakiness, while the butter gives it
flavour. If you don't have lard, you can simply replace
it with an equal quantity of butter. Of course it goes
without saying that you can just as easily buy your
pastry from the supermarket.

Preheat oven to 200°C/400°F/Gas Mark 6.

1. To make the pastry, either put the flour, a pinch of salt
    and the fats in a food processor and pulse until you get
    fine breadcrumbs, or rub it together by hand in a bowl.
    Add 1–2 tablespoons of water until the pastry comes
    together into a ball. You don't want it too crumbly, as it
    will be harder to roll. Chill the pastry for 15 to 30 minutes
    in the fridge, loosely wrapped in some cling film.
2. On a floured worktop, roll out the pastry to about the
    thickness of a pound coin (roughly 5mm). Use it to line
    your tart tin, pressing the pastry down into the base
    and pushing it gently up the sides. Don't trim the pastry
    at this stage – leave it to flop over the edges of the tin.
    Prick the pastry all over with a fork and then line it with
    greaseproof paper. Add baking beans or rice and bake the
    pastry 'blind' in the oven for 15 minutes. This will give it
    a nice crisp base and stop it shrinking when you cook it
    with the filling. Remove the beans and paper and cook

it for another 5 minutes or so to lightly brown the base. Remove from the oven and turn down the temperature to 180°C/350°F/Gas Mark 4.

3. To make the filling, bring a large pan of salted water to the boil and blanch the Swiss chard or broccoli for 3 to 4 minutes. Drain it well, removing as much liquid as possible. Squeeze over a little lemon juice and toss together.

4. Mix the chard or broccoli with the cheese and sprinkle it over the cooked pastry case. Stir together the eggs and single cream, season with a little salt and pepper and grate in a little nutmeg. Pour the mixture into the pastry case over the greens. Give the side of the tart tin a little tap to even out the surface.

5. Bake for around 30 minutes until the tart is golden brown on top and just set – a slight wobble in the middle is good, not least because the tart will carry on cooking inside as it cools down.

6. Using a sharp knife at a 30-degree angle to the rim of the tart tin, gently cut away the extra pastry hanging over the edge. This will give you a lovely clean and straight finish. You can serve this tart warm or chilled.

Jewelled lamb pilau

Serves 2 adults and 2 children

750g diced lamb (shoulder is ideal)

2 garlic cloves, roughly chopped

2.5cm cube of fresh ginger, sliced

½ stick of cinnamon

1 teaspoon green cardamom pods

1 teaspoon coriander seeds

1 bay leaf

1 teaspoon black peppercorns

Salt

Vegetable oil

1 onion, sliced

2 tablespoons plain yoghurt

For the rice

250g basmati rice, rinsed well

½ teaspoon turmeric

50g golden raisins or sultanas

25g dried goji berries, barberries or cranberries

Seeds from 1 small pomegranate (or 100g prepared pomegranate seeds)

A handful of coriander leaves (optional)

I always say that my recipes are very forgiving with regards to the ingredients I suggest using and that they won't fall down if you are missing one or two. That said, pork ribs are never going to work without, well, pork ribs, and in this recipe, the pomegranate is surprisingly central, as it add a huge amount of flavour. The fact that both my children could quite happily live on pomegranate alone is, of course, a bonus. It is very easy (and much cheaper) to deseed a pomegranate yourself. Just cut it in half and, over a large bowl of water, whack the skin with a wooden spoon. All the seeds will come out and sink to the bottom of the water. Any pith will just float to the top. Be careful though: pomegranate juice is the most stainy thing I have ever come across. There's no point in even trying to get it out of your white T-shirt if you splash yourself with it. If you prefer, chicken will work in place of the lamb here and, if you don't want to use the individual dried spices, a tablespoon or two of your favourite curry powder will be a good substitute.

1. Put the lamb in a large casserole along with the garlic, ginger, spices and peppercorns. Season with salt and cover with water. Bring to the boil and use a spoon to skim off any scum that has formed on the surface. Cover with the lid, turn down the heat and simmer for about 30 minutes, until the lamb is tender.

2. Reserving the cooking liquid, strain the lamb through a sieve, getting rid of as many of the spices as possible. Keep the lamb to one side in a bowl.

3. Heat some vegetable oil in the same casserole over a medium heat and cook the onion until it is golden brown. Mix the lamb with the yoghurt, then add it to the casserole and stir until it is a lovely brown colour.

4. Add the rice, along with the turmeric. You need 650ml liquid in total, so use the reserved cooking liquid and make up the rest with water. Pour in the liquid, give it a good stir, and keep cooking until the rice has absorbed most of the water. This will take about 20 minutes. When you are ready to serve, stir in the raisins and berries and sprinkle with the pomegranate seeds and coriander leaves.

Chicken pot pie with mushroom and tarragon

Serves 2 adults and 2 children

You will need a deep 20 x 30cm baking dish or pie dish

Olive oil

A very large knob of butter

2 leeks, sliced into rounds

1 carrot, cut into small cubes

250g white or chestnut mushrooms, halved

600–650g skinless chicken breasts or combination of breasts and thighs, cut into small chunks

A large sprig of tarragon

1 bay leaf

Salt and freshly ground black pepper

50g plain flour, plus extra for dusting

50ml white wine

250ml chicken stock or water

150ml milk

50ml single cream

100g frozen peas

Flour, for dusting

500g block puff pastry

1 egg, beaten

If you've never made one before, I know a pie can seem a bit daunting. But they really aren't at all tricky. This recipe is basically a simple chicken casserole, topped with puff pastry. Easy! If you need to make your food dairy-free, you can replace the milk and cream with more stock or water; because of the flour in the sauce, you will still get a relatively 'creamy' consistency.

Preheat your oven to 190°C/375°F/Gas Mark 5.

1. Heat the oil and butter in a large saucepan and cook the leeks, carrots and mushrooms for a few minutes until the carrots start softening around the edges.
2. Add the chicken along with the tarragon sprig and bay leaf. Season with salt and pepper and keep stirring until the chicken is lightly browned.
3. Sprinkle over the flour and give everything a good stir, then pour in the wine and continue to mix well.
4. Gradually add the stock or water, followed by the milk and finally the cream. Keep stirring until you have a thickened sauce, slightly lighter than Béchamel consistency – like a thin custard.
5. Add the peas and then pour everything into a pie dish.
6. Flour your work surface and roll out the block of pastry to the size of your pie dish. You want it to be around 5mm thick.

7. Dampen the rim of your pie dish with water and place the pastry over the pie (trying to avoid it actually touching the filling). Trim away any excess around the edge and then press down around the rim, crimping if you wish. Brush with the beaten egg and bake for 40 to 45 minutes, until the pastry is golden brown and puffed up.

8. Serve immediately. In my house, this goes on the table with mash.

Malaysian spiced beef (beef rendang)

Serves 2 adults and 2 children

For the curry paste

8 dried red Kashmiri chillies, deseeded and soaked for 15 minutes in warm water

1 teaspoon cumin seeds

1 teaspoon coriander seeds

3cm cube of fresh ginger, chopped

5 garlic cloves, chopped

1 small onion or 2 shallots, finely chopped

1 lemongrass stalk, tough outer leaves removed, chopped

1 teaspoon turmeric

A while back on the radio food programme I present, we had a lovely guest called Endang and she made an equally lovely beef curry called a rendang. As you can imagine, I had much fun talking about Endang's rendang, the most poetic dish we have ever had on the show. This is not her recipe but the ethos is the same: simple, gentle spices marry with coconut to create a mild and creamy coconut sauce. Please don't be put off by the ingredients list; it's the depth of flavour that will make the curry a favourite in your house. That said, as with all my recipes, the dish will not fall down if it is missing a few components. If you have a slow cooker, this recipe is particularly well suited to using one. Because of the slightly longer ingredients list, I am using 1kg of beef to make full use of any extra effort in getting the spices together – this dish will freeze beautifully. The Kashmiri chillies in the paste are very mild. If you can't find them, you can substitute them with any others you know to be mild or with half a teaspoon of ground red chilli and 1 teaspoon sweet paprika.

1. Put all the paste ingredients in a small blender with around 50ml water. Blitz until you have a smooth paste, adding a splash more water if necessary. Alternatively, you can use a pestle and mortar.
2. Toast the coconut in a large, dry casserole on a medium to high heat until it is a light golden brown colour. Remove it from the pan and set to one side in a bowl.
3. Heat the oil in the same casserole and fry the beef, stirring constantly, until it is lightly browned all over. Depending on the size of your casserole, you may need to do this in a couple of batches – don't overcrowd the pan.

For the curry

50g desiccated coconut

Vegetable oil

1kg stewing steak

1 small stick of cinnamon

1 lemongrass stalk, bruised

1 star anise

400ml coconut milk

1 tablespoon palm sugar or soft light brown sugar

2 tablespoons tamarind paste (Bart does a good one in a jar)

6 Kaffir lime leaves, finely sliced (replace these with a little extra lemongrass if you can't get them in your supermarket)

Cooked rice, to serve

Coriander leaves, to garnish

4. Add the curry paste, the cinnamon stick, lemongrass, star anise, coconut milk, sugar, tamarind paste and lime leaves with about 150ml water. Bring to the boil, then turn the heat down to very low and simmer, uncovered, for about 2 hours, stirring every so often. Keep an eye on it in case it needs a little extra water. The sauce should have reduced and thickened and the meat be meltingly tender.
5. Serve with rice and garnish with coriander leaves.

Saving Your Bacon

All the recipes in this book are frugal in one way or another and so there are many recipes I could have easily slipped into this chapter. I never use expensive ingredients and I try to keep waste to a minimum, and this is reflected in everything I make. Still, the recipes in this chapter go that step further. I have steered clear of using much meat and fish, as the prices of both of these are forever on the rise but, as you will see when you cook these dishes, frugal cooking does not in any way mean boring, flavourless meals.

Bacon, leek, onion and potato boulangère

Pommes boulangère is a superb way of cooking potatoes. Think potato gratin but without any milk or cream. By layering the potatoes with flavoursome leeks, onions and bacon, this simple dish turns into a frugal classic. The leeks and onions are naturally sweet and you don't need to be worried by the presence of the mustard powder – its effect is warming and sweetening and this is in no way a spicy dish. Perfect for a chilly autumnal evening, hunks of crusty bread with some real butter are all this needs to become a true family favourite.

Serves 2 adults and 2 children

1 large knob of butter

3 white onions, halved and thinly sliced

400g unsmoked lean bacon, chopped (as much fat removed as possible)

1 large leek, washed and cut into 1cm slices

5 large potatoes, peeled and cut into 3mm slices

Mustard powder, to taste

1 bay leaf

1L chicken or vegetable stock (because of the flavour from the bacon and vegetables, you can simply use water if you don't have stock)

Crusty bread, to serve

Preheat your oven to 180°C/350°F/Gas Mark 4.

1. Put a large ovenproof casserole on a medium heat and melt the butter – be careful not to burn it.
2. Put a layer of onions in the bottom of the dish, followed by some bacon, leek and a layer of potatoes.
3. Sprinkle a little mustard powder over the potatoes and then repeat the exact same layering process, seasoning with mustard powder each time. Be sure to pop the bay leaf in too, about halfway up.
4. Make sure your top layer is made up of potato and, when all the ingredients are used up, pour in your stock or water, so that it is just covering the potatoes – you may not need it all.
5. Put the casserole dish in the oven and cook for 1 to 1½ hours. It is ready when all the potatoes are soft through (a skewer is a good way of checking the potatoes in the middle).
6. Ladle it out and serve with the crusty bread.

Braised sausages with a butterbean mash

Our summer holiday in 2013 resulted in a new nickname for my daughter, Matilda. Her insistence on asking for mashed potatoes every single time we went out for supper meant she was henceforth known as, you've guessed it, Mash. This 'bangers and mash' recipe has two nice twists to it. First, the braising liquid makes a perfect onion gravy, rather than making it separately. And, secondly, to make a change from mashed potato (don't worry, Matilda loves this too), I am serving the sausages with a butterbean mash. It is slightly lighter than mashed potatoes and is also a particularly useful addition to your cooking repertoire if you have low GI dietary requirements. I have made this recipe with vegetarian sausages too, and it worked beautifully.

1. In a large, deep frying pan or casserole, heat the olive oil on a medium heat and brown the sausages all over. Then take them out and leave them to one side.
2. Add the onions and thyme and cook for about 5 minutes until the onions are soft.
3. Stir in the flour, turn up the heat a little, add the red wine (or water) and then the stock.
4. Return the sausages to the pan, season well with salt and pepper, turn down the heat and simmer until the sausages are cooked through. This will probably take 15 to 20 minutes.
5. While the sausages are simmering, make the butterbean mash. Heat the olive oil in a saucepan on a low heat, chuck in the garlic and then, after 10 seconds or so, add the butterbeans and season with salt and pepper.
6. Stir in the milk or cream (and the mustard if you are using it) then crush up the beans using the back of a metal spoon. You don't want a totally smooth texture. Serve it alongside the sausages and gravy.

Serves 2 adults and 2 children

For the sausages
1 tablespoon olive
8 large sausages
2 onions, halved and sliced into crescents
½ teaspoon fresh or dried thyme
2 teaspoons plain flour
100ml red wine or water
250ml beef or chicken stock
Salt and freshly ground black pepper

For the butterbean mash
2 tablespoons olive oil
1 garlic clove, crushed
2 x 400g tins butterbeans, rinsed and drained
Salt and freshly ground black pepper
50ml full-fat milk or single cream

Minced beef minchi

This is great grub to fill up a family frugally. Originating from Macau, in China, minchi is a dish of simple flavours and pleasures. A gentle beef ragù, served with potatoes and rice. Traditionally, the potatoes are deep-fried separately, but I prefer to boil mine and add them in at the end. If the thought of having rice and potatoes in the same dish leaves you thinking 'carb overload', don't worry as, somehow, this dish remains light. That said, if you go the full hog and add the traditional fried egg on top, you will definitely be veering into heavy territory!

Serves 2 adults and 2 children

1 large potato, cut into small cubes

Vegetable oil

I onion, finely chopped

3 garlic cloves, crushed

1 teaspoon ground cumin

450g minced beef (or you can use half-and-half of pork and beef)

1 bay leaf

4–5 tablespoon dark soy sauce

A pinch of sugar

Worcester sauce, to taste

Cayenne pepper, to taste (optional)

Cooked rice, to serve

4 fried eggs, to serve (optional)

1. Boil the potato pieces in salted water for 10 minutes until just cooked but not falling apart. It is important they keep their shape. As soon as they are cooked, drain them and cool them down with lots of cold water then set aside. (Alternatively, you can deep-fry them or bake them, drizzled in olive oil, in an oven at 200°C/400°F/Gas Mark 6 for 30 minutes.)

2. Drizzle some oil into a wok or deep frying pan on a medium heat, and fry the onion for 3 to 4 minutes, until just soft.

3. Stir in the garlic and cumin and cook for a further minute.

4. Turn up the heat to high and add the meat, sealing it nicely all over and breaking it up as it cooks.

5. Chuck in the bay leaf and several glugs of soy sauce. Then in goes a pinch of sugar, several generous drops of Worcester sauce, the cayenne pepper, if using, and a splash of water. Cover and leave to simmer for 5 minutes.

6. Serve the beef ragù on some rice, with the potatoes scattered over the top and, for full Macanese authenticity, a fried egg too. Steamed broccoli goes especially well with this.

Smoked haddock, pea and potato gratin

My early memories of smoked haddock are not good. We used to be served a very pungent kedgeree at my infant school which, single-handedly, put me off smoked haddock for many years. Which was a shame because using smoked haddock is a great way of adding oily fish goodness and flavour to any dish. The beauty of this delicious recipe is that the potatoes take the most of tummy-filling strain, meaning you only need a relatively small amount of fish to feed the whole family.

Preheat the oven to 200°C/400°F/Gas Mark 6.

1. Boil the potatoes in salted water for 10 minutes until they are just cooked but not falling apart. Drain them and then run them under lots of cold water. When they are cool enough to handle, peel them and then cut them into 3–4mm slices.
2. Meanwhile, put the haddock in a saucepan, cover with the milk and add the bay leaf and peppercorns. Bring to the boil, then lower the heat and simmer for 1 minute. Take the pan off heat, leave it for 4 to 5 minutes and then strain the milk into a jug or bowl. Discard the bay leaf and peppercorns and flake the fish (removing any skin and bones).
3. Butter your baking dish. Arrange half the potatoes in the bottom of the dish and season with salt and pepper. Cover with the flaked haddock and peas, and season again. Finally, top with the remaining potatoes.
4. Mix the reserved milk with the crème fraîche and pour it over the potatoes. Sprinkle over the cheese (and breadcrumbs, if using) and dot the surface with butter.
5. Bake the gratin in the oven for 15 to 20 minutes, until it is well browned on top. Serve immediately.

Serves 2 adults and 2 children

You will need a 20 x 30cm baking dish

750g waxy potatoes (e.g. Maris Piper or Desiree), left whole and unpeeled

250g smoked haddock fillet

150–200ml milk (enough to cover the fish)

1 bay leaf

1 teaspoon black peppercorns

Butter

Salt and freshly ground black pepper

100g frozen peas

100ml crème fraîche

100g grated Cheddar cheese

50g breadcrumbs (optional)

Sweetcorn and smoked haddock chowder

Smoked haddock lends itself really well to this lovely thick chowder as it adds both texture and flavour to the finished dish – and the same can be said for the sweetcorn too. I would recommend buying un-dyed smoked haddock if you can as I find its flavour to be more gentle than the yellow dyed equivalent. This is perfect winter-warming comfort food and I often make a double or triple batch. It freezes particularly well and acts as an emergency supper after a defrosting blast in the microwave.

Serves 2 adults and 2 children

400g smoked haddock fillet

600ml milk

A large knob of butter

1 small onion, finely chopped

1 garlic clove, crushed

2 leeks, sliced into rings

2 large potatoes, cut into small cubes

340g tin sweetcorn, drained (or frozen equivalent)

50ml single cream (optional)

2 tablespoons finely chopped flat-leaf parsley, to garnish (optional)

1. Put the smoked haddock in a saucepan and cover it with the milk. Add 150ml water, bring to the boil and then remove the pan from heat. Leave everything to cool.
2. Meanwhile, heat the butter in a large saucepan on a medium heat. Cook the onion for 4 to 5 minutes, until it softens. Chuck in the garlic, leeks and potatoes and give it all a good stir.
3. Strain the milk from cooking the fish into a jug, then flake the fish (removing any skin and bones).
4. Pour the milk over the potatoes in a saucepan and simmer until the potatoes are cooked. Mix in the sweetcorn and flaked haddock and gently heat through.
5. Stir in the cream and garnish the chowder with the chopped parsley. Serve immediately with crusty bread.

Root vegetable gratin with ham and cheese

Grab whatever combination of root vegetables you can get your hands on and chuck them into this lovely gratin. All you need to bear in mind is to have the same weight in potatoes. You want the vegetables to be sliced as thinly as possible – a mandolin works well for this, or you can use the slicer part of a grater. Or just use a sharp knife and think 'as thin as possible' when cutting. This gratin can be prepared well in advance then baked later in the day when you are ready to serve it. The dish won't suffer from having the ham left out, making it fully vegetarian too.

Preheat your oven to 180°C/350°F/Gas Mark 4.

1. Peel all the vegetables and slice them as thinly as you can.
2. Rub the garlic all over your baking dish and follow it with a generous coating of butter.
3. Arrange the vegetables in layers in the gratin dish, seasoning each layer with salt and pepper and sprinkling with the ham and crushed fennel seeds as you go.
4. Mix together the milk, cream and egg and pour it over the vegetables.
5. Top with the cheese and breadcrumbs and bake in the oven for 50 minutes to 1 hour, until the vegetables are all cooked through. A skewer is a good way of checking the potatoes in the middle.

Serves 2 adults and 2 children

You will need a 20 x 30cm baking dish

500g root vegetables (a mixture of one or more of carrot, swede, celeriac, parsnip, turnip, sweet potato and squash or pumpkin)

500g potatoes

1 garlic clove, cut in half

Butter

Salt and freshly ground black pepper

100g ham, cut into cubes or small pieces

2 teaspoons fennel seeds, crushed

200ml milk

300ml single cream

1 egg, beaten

100g grated cheese (Cheddar works well, as always, but you can vary it with any hard, grate-able cheese)

50g breadcrumbs (optional)

Vegetable tagine with couscous

Serves 2 adults and 2 children

2 tablespoons vegetable or olive oil

1 onion, chopped

2 garlic cloves, crushed

1 tablespoon ground cumin

1 tablespoon ground coriander

½ teaspoon ground ginger

1 teaspoon ground cinnamon

3 large carrots, cut into 1.5cm chunks

1 large courgette, cut into 1.5cm chunks

1 small butternut squash, cut into 1.5cm chunks

1 red pepper, deseeded and cut into small cubes

400g tin chickpeas, rinsed and drained

400g tin chopped tomatoes

50g dates, pitted and chopped up

A drizzle of honey

Salt and freshly ground black pepper

During the autumn and winter months, I make a version of this tagine, in one form or another, almost every week. This was always a bit of a risk with Matilda when she was very little, as couscous, covered in tomato, has a wonderful habit of ending up absolutely bloody everywhere when being eaten by a small child armed with a spoon. Still, it is one of our go-to recipes so we always trade off the fear of the mess with the knowledge that the children will love their dinner and get loads of great minerals to boot. In our house, Archie loves the added chickpeas, but Matilda meticulously picks them out one by one and refuses to eat them! We often have leftovers from the quantities given here.

1. Heat the oil in a large saucepan on a medium heat and throw in the onion. Cook, stirring, for 3 to 4 minutes, until just softened.
2. Add the garlic and all the spices, and cook for a further minute, stirring all the time.
3. Chuck in all the vegetables and chickpeas and coat them in the onions and spices.
4. Pour in the chopped tomatoes, add the dates, a squirt of honey and enough water to just cover the contents of the saucepan. Season with salt and pepper and simmer for 25 to 30 minutes until all the vegetables are nice and soft and the tagine is not watery. If you feel the sauce is getting a little dry, simply add some extra water; conversely, if it seems a little liquid at the end, keep simmering for a few more minutes.

5. About 10 minutes before the end of the tagine cooking time, make the couscous. Heat a saucepan and put the dry couscous in it, stirring so it heats up (this seals it and helps make it nice and flaky). Drizzle over some olive oil and add the butter. Season with salt and pepper and give it a stir. Remove the pan from the heat and allow it to cool for a minute. Pour over the water, standing back a little in case it bubbles up. Cover and leave the couscous to steam for 5 to 6 minutes. Fluff up with a fork just before serving and mix through the herbs, if using.

For the couscous

250g couscous (pour it into a cup and then measure out exactly the same volume in water)

Olive oil

25g butter, broken into small lumps

Salt and freshly ground black pepper

Mixture of chopped mint and flat-leaf parsley (optional)

Mushroom and spring greens barley 'risotto'

Serves 2 adults and 2 children

Olive oil

Butter

250g mushrooms, sliced or quartered (chestnut mushrooms give the best flavour)

1 onion, finely diced

25g dried mushrooms, soaked in a little water (optional)

3 garlic cloves, crushed

1 teaspoon fresh thyme leaves

1 teaspoon fennel seeds, crushed

250g pearl barley

Salt and freshly ground black pepper

1.25L vegetable or chicken stock

250g spring greens (such as Savoy cabbage), shredded

50g freshly grated Parmesan cheese, plus extra to serve

A handful of chopped flat-leaf parsley, to serve

Beware the mistrust you may meet when serving barley! I have served this dish so many times to guests and I can palpably feel their concern at a risotto that is not made with rice. The lovely thing is that this concern quickly dissipates once they realise how lovely and creamy the barley is, with its almost nutty flavour and pasta-like texture. The other bonus, that they are probably not spotting, is that barley is ridiculously cheap. Barley also has that indescribable quality of just feeling comforting and warming to eat – perfect for a chilly after-school evening. Although this is very much a frugal dish, you can add a bag of dried mushrooms for extra flavour, although this will obviously make the dish a little more expensive.

1. Heat a glug of olive oil and a knob of butter in a deep pan or saucepan and fry the fresh mushrooms over a high heat for a couple of minutes until they are nicely browned. Don't pack the pan, but try to keep them in roughly one layer, otherwise the mushrooms will start to 'steam'. You may need to do this in a couple of batches. Remove the mushrooms from the pan and set aside.

2. Add a bit more butter and oil to the pan and soften the onion for 3 to 4 minutes. Meanwhile, if you are using dried mushrooms as well, drain them now, saving the soaking liquid but making sure there isn't any grit at the bottom. Chop them roughly.

3. Add the garlic, thyme and fennel seeds to the onion, stir for a couple of minutes and then pour in the pearl barley. Mix well and season with salt and pepper. Stir in the chopped dried mushrooms, if using.

4. Pour over the stock and the mushroom soaking liquid, if using. Bring to the boil, then turn down the heat and simmer for 15 minutes.
5. Mix in the cooked fresh mushrooms and the spring greens and simmer for 5 minutes. The barley will now have a risotto-like texture. If it is still a little liquid, let it cook for a few extra minutes.
6. Finally, stir in a large slice of butter and the Parmesan. Serve with extra grated cheese and the chopped parsley.

Saving Your Bacon

Cheese and sweetcorn pudding

Delicious family food doesn't get much simpler than this recipe.
This lovely savoury pudding puffs up and feeds your family with
ingredients that are most likely already in your kitchen and which
will have cost you next to nothing. It is lovely served with sliced
ham, or you can add some diced ham or fried bacon to the mix
just before putting it in the oven. Any leftovers can be kept in the
fridge for a couple of days and reheated.

**Serves 2 adults and
2 children**

You will need a deep 20 x
30cm baking dish or pie dish

Butter

500g sweetcorn, either
tinned or frozen

250g grated mature
Cheddar cheese

2 large eggs

A pinch of cayenne pepper

2 tablespoons plain flour
or fine cornmeal

Salt and freshly ground
black pepper

Preheat your oven to 160°C/325°F/Gas Mark 3.

1. Butter your baking dish and then melt 25g butter in a
   small saucepan or in a dish in the microwave.
2. Purée about two-thirds of the sweetcorn in a food
   processor or blender, then add two-thirds of the cheese,
   both eggs, the cayenne pepper, melted butter and flour
   and blitz again. Season with salt and pepper.
3. Stir in the remaining sweetcorn and cheese, and then
   pour the mixture into the buttered ovenproof dish.
4. Bake for 40 to 45 minutes until the pudding is a deep
   golden brown on top. Serve with some lightly steamed
   greens, such as broccoli.

Rice and peas (risi e bisi)

How can something so simple be so very tasty? This classic Venetian money-saving dish does exactly what Italian food always does so well: it uses a few tasty ingredients, prepares them without fuss and creates a totally delicious dish. This is not a risotto, although the cooking technique is not far from the traditional risotto method. It is more of a warming, soupy dish and should be able to be eaten with a spoon. Lovely.

1. On a medium heat, melt 50g of the butter in a large saucepan with a little drizzle of olive oil.
2. Throw in your chopped onion and continue to cook for 4 to 5 minutes until it softens nicely and starts to colour a little.
3. Next add the peas, mixing them well with the onions.
4. Pour in the stock, simmer for a couple of minutes and then add the rice. Give it a good stir and then leave it to simmer until the rice is just cooked and it is still very soupy. This will take 15 to 20 minutes. Make sure you check it regularly. If it looks as though it is getting a little dry, add some hot water. Remember, you don't want it to thicken like a risotto.
5. When the rice is cooked, beat in the remaining butter and the Parmesan, season with salt and pepper then stir in the parsley if you are using it.
6. Serve with extra grated Parmesan and some crusty bread.

Serves 2 adults and 2 children

75g butter

Olive oil

1 onion, finely chopped

250g frozen peas (or fresh if you have good ones)

750ml good-quality chicken or vegetable stock

200g risotto rice

2 good handfuls of freshly grated Parmesan cheese, plus extra to serve

Salt and freshly ground black pepper

1 tablespoon finely chopped flat-leaf parsley (optional)

Saving Your Bacon

Honey glazed chicken wings

Serves 2 adults and 2 children

12–16 chicken wings, pointed tips removed (you can cut the wings in half if you want to)

Salt and freshly ground black pepper

For the marinade

1 small onion, finely chopped

2 garlic cloves, crushed

2.5cm cube of fresh ginger, grated

1 tablespoon vegetable oil

50ml dark soy sauce

For the glaze

1 tablespoon honey

1 teaspoon Dijon or wholegrain mustard

1 tablespoon ketchup or tomato purée

1 teaspoon white wine vinegar

1 tablespoon dark soy sauce

Salt and freshly ground black pepper

If you have a friendly local butcher, he will sell you a bag of chicken wings for next to nothing. If not, you should be able to find the wings for this recipe in your local supermarket for just a few pounds. These sticky-fingered wings have a double layer of flavour: first with a simple ginger and garlic marinade and then thanks to the sticky glaze they are baked in. If you are really pushed for time, add the ginger and garlic to the glaze and make the wings without marinating them first.

1. First blitz the marinade ingredients in a food processor or blender until they are nice and smooth. If you don't have a food processor or blender, try to ensure that the ingredients are finely chopped and grated and perhaps give them a whack in a pestle and mortar.
2. Put the chicken wings in bowl then pour over your marinade ingredients. Leave the wings for as long as possible – overnight is best but an hour will be sufficient.
3. Now preheat your oven to 200°C/400°F/Gas Mark 6. Drain the marinade from the chicken.
4. Mix together the glaze ingredients and pour them over the wings. This is a messy job best done with your hands.
5. Season the wings with salt and pepper, then arrange them in one layer in a baking dish.
6. Cook the wings for around 30 minutes, turning them every so often, until they are well browned and cooked through. Serve hot or cold.

Mussels with bacon and garlic broth

I am not going to lie to you, this was one of a handful recipes that I filed in a category loosely entitled 'controversial'. These mussels are totally tasty and lightning quick to make. I guess you are either going to have children who love mussels or who hate them; I have one of each in my house. If the children don't like them, I'd still recommend cooking this dish as an adult treat. It is worth noting that a bag of fresh mussels (when they are in season) is an inexpensive addition to your shopping trolley.

Remember the golden rule when dealing with mussels: before cooking, discard any that are open and after they have cooked, discard any that haven't opened.

1. Heat a glug of olive oil and a big knob of butter in a large pan on a medium heat. Fry the bacon and leek until the bacon is starting to crisp and brown.
2. Stir in the garlic and cook for a further minute or two – be careful not to burn it.
3. Pour in the cider, bring to the boil and season lightly with salt and pepper.
4. Add all the mussels, cover the pan and cook for 3 to 4 minutes, shaking regularly, until they have all opened. Discard any that are still closed.
5. Pour in the cream and gently turn over the mussels to coat and combine everything.
6. Sprinkle over lots of parsley and serve with hunks of buttered bread – or go Belgian and serve with lots of chips. Or both!

Serves 2 adults and 2 children

Olive oil

Butter

100g chopped bacon or lardons

1 leek, sliced into rounds

4 garlic cloves, crushed

100ml cider

Salt and freshly ground black pepper

1kg mussels, cleaned

100ml cream

Fresh flat-leaf parsley, to serve

Egg and potato curry with flatbreads

I often make this the day after we've eaten new potatoes with our supper. A kilo of new potatoes (the standard supermarket packet weight) is difficult to use up in one go and so this dish provides the perfect opportunity to make sure none is wasted. The curry sauce is a great one to have in your cooking locker, as it works with almost any meat or vegetables you care to add to it. And the flatbreads are fun to make, easy to get right and the ingredients cost pennies.

Serves 2 adults and 2 children

For the flatbreads *

250g strong white bread flour, plus extra to dust

2 teaspoons dried instant yeast

1 teaspoon salt

1 teaspoon sugar

1 tablespoon plain yoghurt

4 tablespoons olive oil

For the curry

1 tablespoon vegetable oil

1 teaspoon cumin seeds

1 onion, finely chopped

2cm cube of fresh ginger, grated

2 garlic cloves, crushed

1 tablespoon of your favourite curry powder

400g tin chopped tomatoes

4 tablespoons plain yoghurt

Salt and freshly ground black pepper

200g new potatoes, boiled and cut into chunks if large

4 hard-boiled eggs

100g frozen peas

A handful of fresh coriander leaves, to serve

1. To make the flatbreads, mix the flour with the yeast, salt and sugar in a large bowl. Add the yoghurt, olive oil and 100ml water. Form into a dough with your hands, then knead lightly for around 5 minutes until smooth. Cover the bowl with cling film and leave the dough to rise in a warm place for about an hour until doubled in size. After about 45 minutes, make a start on the curry.

2. Heat the oil in a large saucepan over a high heat. Add the cumin seeds and when they start to splutter, add the chopped onion and cook for 4 to 5 minutes until soft. Add the ginger, garlic and curry powder and cook for 2 minutes.

3. Stir in the tomatoes and yoghurt and season with salt and pepper. Leave to simmer for 15 minutes.

4. When the dough has finished rising, lightly flour your worktop. Divide the dough into equal-sized balls. You can make 4 large, 8 medium or 12 small flatbreads with this quantity. Roll out the balls to a thickness of roughly 3mm.

* you can also buy some or use plain pittas

5. Heat a frying pan with no oil in it over a medium heat and cook the flatbreads one at a time in the pan. The flatbreads will need no more than thirty seconds on each side and are ready when they start to puff up a little. Keep the cooked flatbreads on a plate and cover them in foil to keep them warm.

6. While you are cooking the flatbreads, chuck the potatoes, eggs and peas into the curry, lower the heat a little and simmer for a couple of minutes until everything is warmed through.

7. Stir through the chopped coriander leaves and serve immediately with the flatbreads.

Spinach and sweet potato dhal

Serves 2 adults and 2 children

1 tablespoon vegetable oil

1 teaspoon cumin seeds

1 onion, finely chopped

A small bunch of coriander, stems and leaves separated, stems chopped

2 garlic cloves, finely chopped

2.5cm cube of fresh ginger, grated

1 teaspoon turmeric

1 tablespoon curry powder (see below)

1 large sweet potato (or 1 small butternut squash), cut into small cubes

250g dried red lentils

200g tin chopped tomatoes or chopped fresh tomatoes

Salt

2 tablespoons grated block coconut cream

8 cubes of frozen spinach (or 100g fresh spinach)

A squeeze of lime juice

Chilli powder or cayenne pepper, to taste

Lentils rock. They are so cheap (especially if you hunt them out in the specialist food aisle) and they are remarkably filling. In many ways, they are the ultimate frugal ingredient and can be used to bulk up most casseroles and stews. This dhal has a lovely creaminess, enhanced by the use of creamed coconut. Creamed coconut is a great ingredient to have in your cupboard because it keeps very well if stored in a dry airtight container. It also makes a good substitute for coconut milk if a recipe calls for less than a full tin (however, don't confuse it with the thick liquid coconut cream). I have given you a recipe for your own curry powder in case you fancy making one. Alternatively, just use 1½ or 2 tablespoons of your favourite curry powder. If your family is spinach averse, replace it with peas or beans.

1. If you are making your own curry powder, toast the spices in a dry frying pan for a minute or two – be careful not to burn them. Remove them from the pan and leave them to cool, then grind them in a spice grinder or using a pestle and mortar.

2. Heat the vegetable oil in a saucepan on a medium heat. Add the cumin seeds and when they splutter, stir in the onion and cook for 4 to 5 minutes until soft.

3. Mix the chopped coriander stems into the onion, along with the garlic, ginger, turmeric and curry powder.

4. Add the sweet potato (or squash) and the lentils, stirring until everything is well coated in the spices. Pour in the tomatoes, followed by 750ml water. Season with a little salt, bring to the boil and then simmer until the lentils are soft. This will take around 20 minutes.

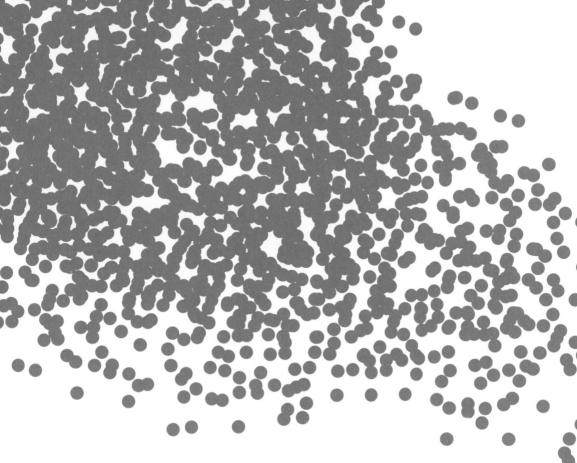

5. Stir in the grated creamed coconut and the spinach and simmer for 2 minutes.
6. Taste, and season with a little extra salt if you think it needs it. Squeeze in a little lime juice.
7. Sprinkle the coriander leaves over the dhal and serve with flatbreads (see page 66) or basmati rice. If you want some extra heat, stir through the chilli powder or cayenne pepper at the table.

For the curry powder

½ stick of cinnamon

1 bay leaf

2 cloves

4 green cardamom pods

1 teaspoon coriander seeds

1 teaspoon cumin seeds

1 teaspoon fenugreek seeds

1 teaspoon black peppercorns

Simple chicken soup and my mum's *kneidlach*

Serves 2 adults and 2 children

For the chicken soup

Olive oil

1 large onion, chopped

3 carrots, chopped

3 sticks of celery, chopped

1 tbsp plain flour

1.5L chicken stock

A couple of good handfuls of leftover cooked chicken, shredded (around 300g)

100g vermicelli pasta, crushed into short strands

A handful of chopped flat-leaf parsley, to serve

For the kneidlach

25g margarine or butter

1 medium white onion, finely chopped

1 large egg

100ml water

125g medium matzo meal (I like Rakusen's)

Jewish food is traditionally thrifty, especially the kind of food my great-grandparents would have made when they were newly arrived immigrants in the East End of London. Suppertime was all about feeding many mouths as wholesomely and as cheaply as possible, using leftovers and simple ingredients. Chopped liver is a prime example, as is perhaps the best-known Jewish dish of all: chicken soup. Throughout my whole life, my Grandma, my Nanny and my mum have plied me with chicken soup, certain in the knowledge that it is not called Jewish penicillin for no reason. The centrepiece of chicken soup is *kneidlach*, the hearty and filling soup dumplings. It took several stages of delicate negotiation to get my mum to give me her *kneidlach* recipe (I may or may not have mentioned it was going in the book!) but they are a frugal favourite in our family and fit perfectly into this chapter so I had to have them. My mum always makes the full-length chicken soup, cooked slowly using chicken bones but I have opted for a cheat's version here using readymade chicken stock. If you make too many kneidlach, you can freeze them after cooking them. They are brilliant in bowls of tinned tomato soup. Matzo meal is very widely available in supermarkets and doubles up as excellent breadcrumbs too, so it's well worth having a bag of it in your store cupboard.

1. Heat a glug of olive oil in a large saucepan on a medium heat. Add the onion, carrot and celery and fry for 5 to 6 minutes until they start to soften.
2. Chuck in the flour and stir it into the vegetables.
3. Pour in the chicken stock and bring to the boil. Turn down the heat and leave the soup to simmer for 20 minutes.

4. Meanwhile, make the *kneidlach*. Melt the margarine or butter in a pan on medium heat and gently fry the onion for 5 minutes until soft. Transfer the onion and the fat in the pan to a bowl and stir in the egg and water.

5. Add the matzo meal and mix together well. You are looking for a firm but not too dry consistency. You can always add a little extra matzo meal if necessary but be careful it doesn't become too hard. (This mixture can be kept in the fridge, covered in cling film, for up to a day.)

6. Bring a saucepan of water to the boil. Roll pieces of the *kneidlach* dough, each about the size of a walnut, between your hands.

7. Carefully drop the *kneidlach* into the boiling water and cook for 10 minutes.

8. Once the soup has been simmering for 20 minutes and the vegetables have softened, add the shredded chicken and the vermicelli. Cook for a further 3 to 4 minutes before finally adding the *kneidlach*.

9. Mix in the chopped parsley and serve the soup immediately with some crusty bread.

Speed of Night

When time is of the essence (I don't know about you, but it very rarely isn't of the essence in my house), these dishes will ensure that food is on the table quickly and without fuss. As well as the obvious pastas and stir-fries, I have included two pressure cooker meals. They can also be made conventionally, but who isn't tempted by a risotto that takes only 5 minutes to cook?

Salmon, courgette and tomato linguine

All hail the wonderful tomato purée! OK, that is probably a little over the top but I do think tomato purée is terribly underrated, especially when it comes to pasta sauces. Maybe it's just that we have been a little bit spoilt by passatas, chopped tomatoes and sauces in jars. The thing is, tomato purée creates a lovely, dry, almost sticky red sauce when stirred into pasta and that's why I often use it at home for the quickest pasta sauce imaginable. It is also very cheap indeed, so it really would be a shame not to have it among your staples. Here, I am jazzing it up a little with courgette, red onion and a couple of fillets of salmon, which are cooked in the pasta water, meaning this pasta dish is on the table in 15 minutes.

Serves 2 adults and 2 children

350g linguine

2 x 170g salmon fillets, skin removed

Olive oil

1 red onion, cut in half and finely sliced

1 courgette, cut into 1cm cubes

3 garlic cloves, chopped

200g tomato purée

Salt and freshly ground black pepper

A good handful of freshly grated Parmesan cheese, to serve

1. Cook the pasta in a large saucepan of salted boiling water according to the packet instructions. With 7 minutes of the cooking time left, drop in the salmon fillets.
2. Meanwhile, pour a glug of olive oil into a large frying pan on a medium heat and gently fry the onion and courgette for 5 to 6 minutes, until soft. Add the garlic, stirring for a further minute.
3. Squirt in all the tomato purée, season with salt and pepper and keep the 'sauce' moving around the pan, stirring it occasionally. You will find that the vegetables stick together in a bit of a tomato purée ball. Don't worry: they will be stirred out once the pasta is added.
4. Drain the pasta and rinse under cold water. Flake the salmon and then mix the pasta and salmon into the vegetables in the pan. Keep mixing until the pasta is heated through and fully covered in tomato.
5. Serve immediately with the freshly grated Parmesan.

Greek-style lamb chops with butterbeans

Lamb chops are not the cheapest cuts of meat but when we do have them as a treat, they are always wolfed down, full carnivore style. It may seem as though two lemons is a lot but the recipe does need them, both for flavour and also to tenderise the meat slightly. You can use any kind of bean here (such as cannellini or flageolet), but I use butterbeans, as they are the closest to the kind of giant Greek beans you may well have enjoyed on your Mediterranean holidays.

Serves 2 adults and 2 children

12–16 small lamb chops or cutlets

Juice and zest of 2 lemons

4 garlic cloves, roughly chopped

A good pinch each of dried thyme and oregano

Olive oil

Salt and freshly ground black pepper

For the butterbeans

Olive oil

1 onion, finely chopped

1 bulb of fennel, finely chopped

1 garlic clove, crushed

4 tomatoes, chopped

A pinch of sugar

A pinch of ground cinnamon

2 tablespoons chopped flat-leaf parsley

400g tin butterbeans, rinsed and drained

1. Put the lamb chops in a large bowl or a bag (make sure it doesn't have any holes in it!). Throw in the juice and zest of the lemons, the garlic, herbs and a generous glug of olive oil. Season with salt and pepper, massage the marinade into the meat and leave it to rest for 10 to 15 minutes.
2. For the butterbeans, heat some olive oil in a saucepan, add the onion and fennel and cook for 4 to 5 minutes until they start to soften. Throw in the garlic and cook for a further minute, then follow with the tomatoes, sugar, cinnamon, parsley and butterbeans. Simmer on a low heat while you cook the lamb, but keep an eye on it and add a splash of water if it looks like it's starting to dry out.
3. Drain the lamb chops, brushing off most of the garlic.
4. Cook the chops under a hot grill, on a hot griddle pan or on the barbecue. Depending on the thickness of your meat, you want to cook them for around 4 minutes on each side for medium. Leave them to rest for a minute or two before serving.
5. Crush the beans very lightly with the back of a spoon (you are NOT looking for a mash here) and serve them with the cooked lamb chops.

Smooth cheese and garlic pasta with sun-dried tomatoes (no-cook sauce)

Serves 2 adults and 2 children

1 whole head of garlic, fully intact

Salt and freshly ground black pepper

400g pasta (you can use anything you like, including spaghetti)

Olive oil

200g cream cheese

Zest of 1 lime (yes, that's lime. Trust me on this one)

Around 10 sun-dried tomatoes, in oil, drained and chopped (see below)

A bunch of basil, torn

Freshly grated Parmesan cheese, to serve

I know I say so myself, but this is clever. Cooked garlic has a far more mellow flavour than raw garlic so, for this simple store-cupboard sauce, I cook a whole head of garlic in the boiling pasta water. A head may seem like an awful lot, but boiling it results in a creaminess and a wonderful mild taste that marries beautifully with the cheese. And there's another clever trick here: if you want to avoid the cost of the sun-dried tomatoes, make them yourself, thanks to the brilliant method outlined underneath the recipe. This was given to me by James Harkin, who runs a lovely restaurant called The Alpine, in Bushey. Using the heat of an oven – which you are already using for something else – costs nothing in terms of gas or electricity. It's a brilliant way of saving money, without compromising on flavour.

1. Peel away some of the outer skin of the garlic bulb but go gently – you want it to remain fully intact. Bring a large pan of water to the boil and salt it generously. Throw in the garlic head.
2. Assuming your pasta requires the classic 11 or 12 minutes of cooking time, wait for 5 or 6 minutes before adding it to the boiling water and garlic.
3. With 3 or 4 minutes of the pasta's cooking time remaining, remove the garlic and let it cool down. After a couple of minutes, squish the flesh out of its skin into a bowl. Drizzle with olive oil and add the cream cheese and lime zest. Beat it all together before mixing in the sun-dried tomatoes. Season with salt and pepper.

4. Drain the pasta, reserving a good ladleful of the cooking water, and mix it (while it is still hot) into the sauce. If it seems a bit thick, stir in some of the reserved cooking water a little at a time.
5. Scatter over the torn basil and serve with lots of grated Parmesan.

To make your own sun-dried tomatoes

1. Heat your oven to its highest temperature (for example, after making a roast). Take medium-sized tomatoes and cut them in half. Arrange them on a baking tray. Sprinkle them with salt and drizzle with olive oil. Put them in the hot oven, then immediately turn the oven off. Leave the tomatoes in the oven overnight. They will dry out beautifully. Store them in an airtight container in olive oil, along with some peeled cloves of garlic. They should keep for several weeks.

Wok-braised aubergines with tofu and black bean sauce

I am not ashamed to admit that on a busy day a pack of pre-cut vegetables does the trick very nicely in this recipe. Sometimes life is just too hectic to be chopping up veg. The aubergine is braised, meaning it keeps its shape and holds lots of flavour. It also requires less supervision to braise vegetables than fry them. This dish is absolutely packed with vitamins and the addition of tofu gives this simple stir-fry a lovely texture.

Serves 2 adults and 2 children

2 tablespoons vegetable oil

2 garlic cloves, finely chopped

2cm cube of fresh ginger, finely chopped

2 spring onions, finely sliced

2 medium aubergines, cut into 2–3cm cubes

1 small red or green pepper, deseeded and sliced lengthways

1 carrot, cut into thin batons

1 courgette, cut into thin batons

¼ white cabbage, shredded

100g firm tofu, cut into cubes

3 tablespoons black bean sauce

½ teaspoon sugar

1 teaspoon rice wine vinegar or cider vinegar

A pinch of Chinese five spice

100ml stock or water

A good glug of soy sauce

Salt and freshly ground black pepper

225g fine egg noodles

Coriander leaves, to serve

1. Heat the oil in a wok on your highest heat. Add the garlic, ginger and spring onions and cook for 30 seconds – be careful not to burn the garlic.
2. Add all the vegetables and stir-fry for 3 minutes before throwing in the remaining ingredients (apart from the noodles and coriander leaves).
3. Turn the heat down a little and cook, uncovered, until the vegetables are just tender. This will take around 10 minutes. Keep an eye on the wok and add a splash of water if it looks like it's drying out. Conversely, if you find that the sauce needs reducing further, turn the heat up again for a minute or two.
4. Meanwhile, cook the noodles according to the packet instructions. Drain and serve with the stir-fry and coriander leaves sprinkled over the top.

Wonderful shakshouka

This shakshouka may have to be one of those recipes where I ask you just to trust me. This is always very popular with everyone who eats it, and with good cause. Why do eggs work so well with peppers and tomatoes? I am not sure but, my word, they do! Think of this dish as ratatouille meets a fry-up and you are part of the way to getting a sense of what it is. It is a staple in North Africa, as well as in Israel. And Mexico can lay claim to a similar dish with its huevos rancheros. The lamb is entirely optional, as many shakshouka recipes are vegetarian. If you want a runny egg yolk, use the yoghurt during cooking as described, as it will act as protection for the yolk. If you prefer your yolk to be set, simply add the yoghurt at the end.

1. Heat the olive oil in your large frying pan. Cook the onions and peppers for 5 minutes until they soften, then add the garlic, spices and lamb (if you are using it) and cook for a further minute or so, until the lamb has browned a little all over.
2. Stir in the tomato purée and cook for 2 minutes before adding the tomatoes. Season with salt and pepper, then bring to the boil and simmer for 3 to 4 minutes until the sauce thickens a little.
3. Make 4 wells in the sauce and break an egg into each hole. Spoon yoghurt over each egg yolk, then put the lid on the pan and cook until the whites are set and cooked through – this will take around 5 minutes.
4. Serve with the fresh herbs sprinkled over the top, and lots of crusty fresh bread.

Serves 2 adults and 2 children

You will need a large frying pan with a lid

2 tablespoons olive oil

1 red onion, cut into thin wedges

2 red peppers, deseeded and sliced lengthways

2 garlic cloves, finely chopped

1 teaspoon ground cumin

½ teaspoon paprika

150g lamb mince (optional)

1 tablespoon tomato purée

200g tin chopped tomatoes or chopped fresh tomatoes

Salt and freshly ground black pepper

4 large eggs

4 tablespoons thick Greek yoghurt

Fresh herbs (mint, flat-leaf parsley and coriander all work well), to garnish

Sweet pork and green bean stir-fry

Serves 2 adults and 2 children

225g fine egg noodles

Vegetable oil

500g pork mince

1 onion, finely chopped

2 garlic cloves, crushed

3cm cube of fresh ginger, grated or chopped

1 lemongrass stalk, hard outer layers removed, finely chopped

2 heaped tablespoons soft dark brown sugar

Dark soy sauce

Thai fish sauce

200g green beans, cut in half lengthways (fine ones work best)

A bunch of coriander, chopped

It is no understatement to say that this is in the top five most popular dishes in our house, and has been for some time now. It just has that indefinable x-factor for my children and yet is very simple in its execution. We all have our turn-to dishes that we are able to cook on autopilot and this is one of mine. It is sweet and richly coloured and makes use of very underrated (in my opinion) pork mince. I may be splitting hairs here but I prefer the drier texture of pork mince compared with beef. I also find it has more flavour and it is, of course, a bit kinder on cholesterol levels too. The addition of green beans makes this very much a whole meal in one wok.

1. Cook the noodles according to the packet instructions.
2. Meanwhile, heat a really good drizzle of vegetable oil in a wok or deep frying pan on your highest heat. Add the pork and fry for 3 minutes, breaking it up with your spoon as you go.
3. Throw in the onion, garlic, ginger and lemongrass and continue to stir and cook for 5 to 6 minutes until the onion is soft and the pork is lightly browned all over.
4. Stir in the sugar followed by several good glugs of soy sauce and a few drops of the fish sauce. Continue to stir until everything is a lovely dark brown colour, then add the green beans. Pour in a small glass of water, cover the wok and cook for a further 4 minutes. The sauce should be dry but if it seems at all liquid at this stage, simmer for an extra minute or so with the lid off.
5. Stir in the coriander. Chop the noodles with some scissors to create shorter strands and mix them into the sauce, making sure all the noodles are well covered. Serve immediately.

Matzo brei

Matzos are unleavened bread crackers traditionally
eaten during the Jewish festival of Passover but widely
available all year round in supermarkets. A box will set
you back about a pound. Matzo brei is an ultra-quick
dish, made by soaking broken pieces of matzo in
egg and then frying them in a hot pan. Think of it as
a Jewish take on eggy French toast. This is a true
taste of my childhood that I have passed on to Archie
and Matilda, both of whom regularly request it from
their Nana. Trust me on this one: although you may
be struggling to visualise it, your children will love
it. Feel free to add things to the brei to jazz it up.
Ironically, some crispy bacon would be marvelous!

**Serves 2 adults and
2 children**

300g packet of matzos

2 eggs, beaten

Salt and freshly ground
black pepper

Olive or vegetable oil

1. Boil the kettle. Break the matzos into a bowl –
   each piece should be about 2.5cm square. Cover
   them with boiling water and leave to soak and
   soften for a minute.
2. Drain the matzo pieces in a colander, then return
   them to the bowl and pour over the beaten egg. Mix
   well so all the pieces are nicely coated, then season
   with salt and pepper.
3. Pour a good glug of oil into a large frying pan
   on a medium to high heat and add the soaked
   matzo pieces.
4. Cook for 4 to 5 minutes, stirring all the time. You
   want the matzo pieces to be fairly dry in the middle
   and a little crisp on the edges. Serve immediately.

Chicken, butternut squash and sage risotto

Serves 2 adults and 2 children

Olive oil

Butter

1 leek, finely chopped

4 chicken thighs, skin and bone removed, chopped

1 small butternut squash (approx. 500–600g), cut into small cubes

1 teaspoon dried sage

1 teaspoon lemon zest

300g risotto rice

100ml white wine

750ml chicken stock

Salt and freshly ground black pepper

25g freshly grated Parmesan cheese, plus extra to serve

Basil leaves, to serve

I have memories of my mum using pressure cookers 35 years ago. Back in the day they were a little, shall we say, unreliable and, if truth be told, not always completely safe. Nowadays, they are brilliant contraptions and you can get a very good one fairly inexpensively. Amazingly, they can make a risotto like this one in less than 10 minutes. My friend Catherine Phipps' book, *The Pressure Cooker Cookbook*, is a superb bible for pressure cooking. In truth, it is what inspired me to buy my own and I have not looked back since. If you don't have a pressure cooker, you can bake this risotto in the oven.

1. Heat a good drizzle of olive oil and a large knob of butter in your pressure cooker. Add the leek and cook on a medium heat until soft, then turn up the heat slightly and brown the chicken.
2. Add the butternut squash, sage, lemon zest and risotto rice, stirring to coat in the oil and butter.
3. Turn up the heat to high, pour in the wine and allow it to bubble until evaporated. Pour over the stock, season with salt and pepper then close the lid and bring to high pressure. Cook for 5 minutes then release the pressure quickly.
4. Beat in the Parmesan and 25g butter, put the lid back on and leave the risotto to steam for a couple of minutes or so off the heat to finish cooking.
5. Sprinkle over torn basil leaves and serve with more grated Parmesan.

Note

If you are making this in the oven, use an ovenproof casserole and follow all the steps until the method says to bring the cooker to high pressure. At this stage, simply cover the dish and cook it for 20 to 25 minutes in an oven preheated to 180°C/350°F/Gas Mark 4, until all the water is absorbed and the rice is cooked and creamy. Finish off with butter and cheese and serve as above.

One-pot caponata pasta

This pressure cooker recipe demonstrates quite how quick a pressure cooker meal can be. The pasta cooks with the sauce and, once the lid is closed and the pressure is set to high, it only takes 5 minutes. This is very much a vegetarian pasta dish but there is no reason why you can't add some meat. Bacon, sausage, chorizo, leftover chicken and meatballs are all going to work well here.

Serves 2 adults and 2 children

Olive oil

1 onion, finely chopped

1 carrot, cut into small cubes

1 stick of celery, sliced

1 small aubergine, cut into small cubes

1 courgette, cut into small cubes

2 garlic cloves, chopped

Zest of 1 lemon

1 tablespoon capers

A small handful of olives, sliced

½ teaspoon chilli flakes (optional)

A handful of chopped flat-leaf parsley

300g pasta (such as farfalle, penne or conchiglie)

400g tin chopped tomatoes

2 tablespoons cream cheese

Freshly grated Parmesan cheese and chopped flat-leaf parsley, to serve

1. Heat a good glug of olive oil in the pressure cooker. Add all the vegetables and cook them for 2 minutes on a medium to high heat until they start to brown a little. Throw in the garlic, lemon zest, capers, olives, chilli flakes and parsley and give it all a good stir.
2. Spread an even layer of the pasta over the vegetables and stir lightly. Spoon the tomatoes on top of the pasta without mixing them in. Use the empty tomato tin to add enough water to almost cover the pasta.
3. Close the pressure cooker lid, bring it to high pressure, then turn down the heat and leave it to cook at high pressure for 5 minutes, then release the pressure quickly.
4. Add the cream cheese to thicken the sauce and stir thoroughly. Leave the pasta to sit for a couple of minutes, then serve with freshly grated Parmesan and chopped parsley.

Salt and pepper squid with lemon mayonnaise

My children never cease to surprise me, not least in their willingness to try new foods. We've always encouraged them to be adventurous at mealtimes and, as such, they now have some unusual favourites! Squid is one of those random things that my children really love: easy flavour and simple texture – as long as I never give them the tentacles! This recipe is a simple version of classic fried calamari – lovely with the lemony dipping mayonnaise. You can make your own mayonnaise but you can also simply add the lemon zest and juice, mustard and cayenne pepper to a good-quality shop-bought mayonnaise. I view this more as a snacky supper rather than a full meal for four.

Serves 2 children, with some extra

50g plain flour

Salt and freshly ground black pepper

350g squid rings (you can buy the squid whole or ready-prepared)

Vegetable oil

Lemon wedges, to serve

For the mayonnaise

1 egg yolk

Zest of 1 lemon, plus juice of half

½ teaspoon salt

1 teaspoon Dijon mustard

A pinch of cayenne pepper

300ml vegetable or sunflower oil

1. For the mayonnaise, mix together the egg yolk, lemon zest and juice, salt, mustard and cayenne pepper in a bowl. Start dribbling in the oil very slowly, whisking all the time until it thickens and emulsifies. Once it emulsifies, you can start to add the oil a little more quickly. Continue until all the oil is incorporated. If you prefer not to do this by hand, follow the same instructions but use a food processor.

2. To make the squid, season the flour with salt and pepper in a bowl. Add the squid, mixing thoroughly so that it is well coated in the flour.

3. You are going to deep-fry the squid so heat the vegetable oil in either a large, wide saucepan or in a deep-fat fryer to around 190°C. If you are using a saucepan, be careful not to fill it more than one-third of the way up. To test the oil is hot enough, use a thermometer or drop in a cube of bread – it should fizz and turn golden brown within about 10 to 15 seconds.

4. Shake off any excess flour from the squid and carefully fry in two batches for 1 minute only. The squid should crisp up and turn a light golden brown almost immediately. Drain on kitchen paper.

5. Serve with lemon wedges and the mayonnaise.

Gnocchi with a spinach and creamy tomato sauce

Clever little things, gnocchi. We often eat fried gnocchi in our house. Just fry them in butter in a pan for 3 to 4 minutes on each side and then serve them mixed with pesto, roasted vegetables and Parmesan. For this recipe, I am using the classic cooking method and boiling them. Serve with this simple and quick creamy tomato sauce (with spinach added in for extra goodness) and they will rapidly become one of your store-cupboard essentials. You can jazz up this sauce in all the usual ways: chorizo works nicely and I'd never say no to chucking cooked bacon into a pasta either.

1. Cook the gnocchi according to the packet instructions. Drain it as soon as it is ready, so it doesn't become mushy.
2. While the gnocchi is cooking, drizzle the olive oil into a pan and fry the onion for 3 minutes. Throw in the garlic and stir for a further 30 seconds.
3. Pour in the passata, let the sauce bubble up and then stir in the cream.
4. Mix in the spinach, season with salt and pepper and stir in the cooked gnocchi.
5. Serve with lots of freshly grated Parmesan.

Serves 2 adults and 2 children

500g pack of fresh gnocchi
Olive oil
1 red onion, finely chopped
1 garlic clove, chopped
500ml tomato passata
100–150ml double cream
3 blocks of frozen spinach, defrosted and squeezed (or 250g fresh leaves)
Salt and freshly ground black pepper
Freshly grated Parmesan cheese, to serve

Middle Eastern spiced salmon with orange and mint couscous

Serves 2 adults and 2 children

4 x 150g salmon fillets, skin removed

Olive oil

For the sauce

50ml pomegranate molasses

1 tablespoon honey

1 teaspoon ground cumin

1 teaspoon ground coriander

½ teaspoon ground cinnamon

½ teaspoon harissa paste (a rose-scented one is good here) or some chilli powder, to taste

Salt and freshly ground black pepper

Zest and juice of 1 orange

There are lots of fresh, sweet and typically Middle Eastern flavours on show here. Pomegranate molasses is an excellent addition to any kitchen cupboard and it keeps very well. It has a slightly bitter-sweet flavour and a wonderful aroma. You'll be able to find it in most supermarkets, although you may have to go to the world food aisle. If you have not used pomegranate molasses before, it's the kind of ingredient you will find yourself chucking into all manner of things once you have it close to hand.

1. Mix together the sauce ingredients, apart from the orange juice, with a splash of water until the honey has dissolved. Coat the salmon thoroughly in the sauce and drain any excess back into the bowl (this is not a marinade, so there's no need to leave the salmon in the sauce for any extra time).

2. Rub a large frying pan with olive oil (you want a relatively dry pan, so don't pour the oil in).

3. Heat the pan over a medium heat and cook the salmon fillets on one side for around 5 minutes, then turn them over and cook for a further 4 to 5 minutes, basting with the sauce at intervals.

4. Meanwhile, make the couscous. Heat a saucepan and put the dry couscous in it, stirring so it heats up (this seals it and helps make it nice and flaky). Drizzle over the olive oil and add the butter. Season with salt and pepper and give it a stir. Remove the pan from the heat and allow it to cool for a minute. Pour over the water, standing back a little in case it bubbles up. Cover and leave the couscous to steam for 5 to 6 minutes.

5. By this point, the salmon will be ready – it should give a little when pressed, but should still be slightly pink in the middle. Don't over-cook it, as it will continue to cook when you take it out of the pan. Remove the salmon and set aside. Add any remaining sauce to the pan and pour in the orange juice. Simmer until it has reduced to a very thin syrup.

6. Add the orange zest and juice to the couscous and fluff it up with a fork.

7. Sprinkle over the pistachios, mint and pomegranate seeds and serve alongside the salmon.

For the mint and orange couscous

200g dried couscous (pour it into a cup and then measure out exactly the same volume in water)

1 tablespoon olive oil

25g butter, broken into small lumps

Salt and freshly ground black pepper

Juice of 1 orange and zest of half

2 tablespoons roughly chopped pistachios or pistachio nibs

1 small bunch of mint, torn

Seeds from 1 small pomegranate (or 80g prepared pomegranate seeds)

Grilled chicken breasts with romesco sauce

Serves 2 adults and 2 children

4 chicken breasts, skin removed

Salt and freshly ground black pepper

Olive oil

For the sauce

200g small tomatoes, halved

6 garlic cloves, unpeeled

Salt and freshly ground black pepper

Olive oil

1 slice of stale thick white bread, cut into cubes

15g hazelnuts

1 teaspoon sweet paprika

A pinch of cayenne pepper or chilli flakes

1 tablespoon red wine vinegar or sherry vinegar

This delicious Catalan sauce will instantly become one of your kitchen staples once you have made it. Not only does it go superbly with chicken, it will also go with pretty well anything else, not least of all fish. Roasting the tomatoes for a short period of time enhances and intensifies their flavours and it's then a simple case of blitzing all the sauce ingredients together.

Preheat your oven to 190°C/375°F/Gas Mark 5.

1. First, make a start on the sauce. Put the tomatoes in a shallow roasting dish with the garlic, season with salt and pepper and drizzle with olive oil. Roast in the oven for 10 minutes.
2. Meanwhile, lay each chicken breast between two sheets of cling film or greaseproof paper and flatten them slightly by whacking with a rolling pin.
3. Add the bread and the hazelnuts to the baking dish, drizzle over a little more oil and cook for a further 10 minutes (keeping an eye on it to make sure the bread doesn't burn). When you put the bread and nuts in, you can start cooking the chicken breasts.
4. Season the chicken with salt and pepper, brush with olive oil and cook in a pan on a medium heat for 5 minutes on each side. Leave to one side to rest. If you think the chicken breasts are not fully cooked through, just bung them in the oven for a minute or two when you take out the romesco ingredients.
5. Remove the garlic cloves from their skins and blitz them in a blender or food processor, along with the tomatoes, croûtons, nuts, paprika, cayenne pepper or chilli flakes, the vinegar and an extra glug of olive oil. You want a nice thick paste. If it is too dry, add a little more oil.
6. Serve the chicken with the sauce on top and chips or mash.

Speedy Moroccan tomato and chickpea soup

This is very much the 'Ronseal' of soups. It really does exactly what it says on the tin. It also demonstrates that making soup needn't be a long, laborious task. This turbo-charged version of a classic chickpea soup can be on the table in about 20 minutes. Frugal, simple and extremely quick, plus you can easily add some greens in too – just wilt in some spinach or chard right at the end.

1. Heat a glug of olive oil in a saucepan on a medium heat and fry the onion for 4 to 5 minutes until it is soft.
2. Add the garlic, spices and mint, stirring well to coat the onion thoroughly.
3. Then simply pour in the tomatoes, stock and chickpeas. Season with salt and pepper then bring to the boil and simmer for 10 minutes.
4. Drizzle in half of the lemon juice. Taste it, and if it is tangy enough, stop there. If not, you can add the rest.
5. Serve this soup with lots of parsley or mint on top and spoonfuls of yoghurt swirled through. I like to add some chilli sauce (or harissa) to my bowl, just to give it an extra kick.

Serves 2 adults and 2 children

Olive oil

1 onion, finely chopped

1 carrot, cut into small cubes

1 stick of celery, sliced

1 small aubergine, cut into small cubes

1 courgette, cut into small cubes

2 garlic cloves, chopped

Zest of 1 lemon

1 tablespoon capers

A small handful of olives, sliced

½ teaspoon chilli flakes (optional)

A handful of chopped flat-leaf parsley

300g pasta (such as farfalle, penne or conchiglie)

400g tin chopped tomatoes

2 tablespoons cream cheese

Freshly grated Parmesan cheese and chopped flat-leaf parsley, to serve

Lightly spiced beef noodles with cashew nuts

Serves 2 adults and 2 children

400g steak (sirloin or rump), thinly sliced

225g egg noodles

Sesame oil

Vegetable oil

1 small red onion, thinly sliced

1 red pepper, deseeded and sliced lengthways into thin strips

A small head of broccoli, broken into small florets

130g baby corn

Soy sauce

50g whole roasted cashew nuts

It can be tricky to stir-fry beef, as the quick cooking time means that the cut has to be a very tender one. And if you need a tender cut of beef, it is always going to be more expensive than stewing cuts. However, in this recipe, your marinade will work hard for you, so most types of beef escalope or steak will do the job. Sirloin would be best for flavour, but it's fair to say this would be lost on my children! When you're slicing your beef, make sure you cut across the grain of the meat instead of along it. This will instantly give you more tender meat.

1. Put the steak in a bowl with all the marinade ingredients and a tablespoon of water. Mix to coat and then leave it to marinate for at least 15 minutes. The beef can be left quite happily overnight in the fridge too.
2. Cook the noodles according to the instructions on the packet, then drain them and stir through a little sesame oil.
3. Heat a good glug of vegetable oil in a wok until the work is literally smoking. Fry the beef, stirring constantly and quickly, until it is seared all over. Remove the beef from the wok and keep it to one side in a bowl, complete with its cooking juices.

4. Add a little extra oil to the wok, if necessary, then throw in the onion, pepper, broccoli and baby corn. Cook on a high heat for 2 minutes, then pour over a little water and let it sizzle. Cover the wok, reduce the heat and simmer for 5 minutes.

5. Return the beef to the wok, including any juices. Drizzle in a good glug of soy sauce, then stir through the noodles and the nuts. You can also add a little sesame oil right at the end if you have some to hand. Serve immediately.

For the marinade

2 garlic cloves, finely chopped

1 teaspoon finely chopped fresh ginger

1 teaspoon ground cumin

A generous pinch of curry powder (mild or medium, depending on your preference)

1 tablespoon dark soy sauce, plus extra to serve

2 teaspoons rice wine vinegar or cider vinegar

1 tablespoon sweet chilli sauce

A pinch of sugar

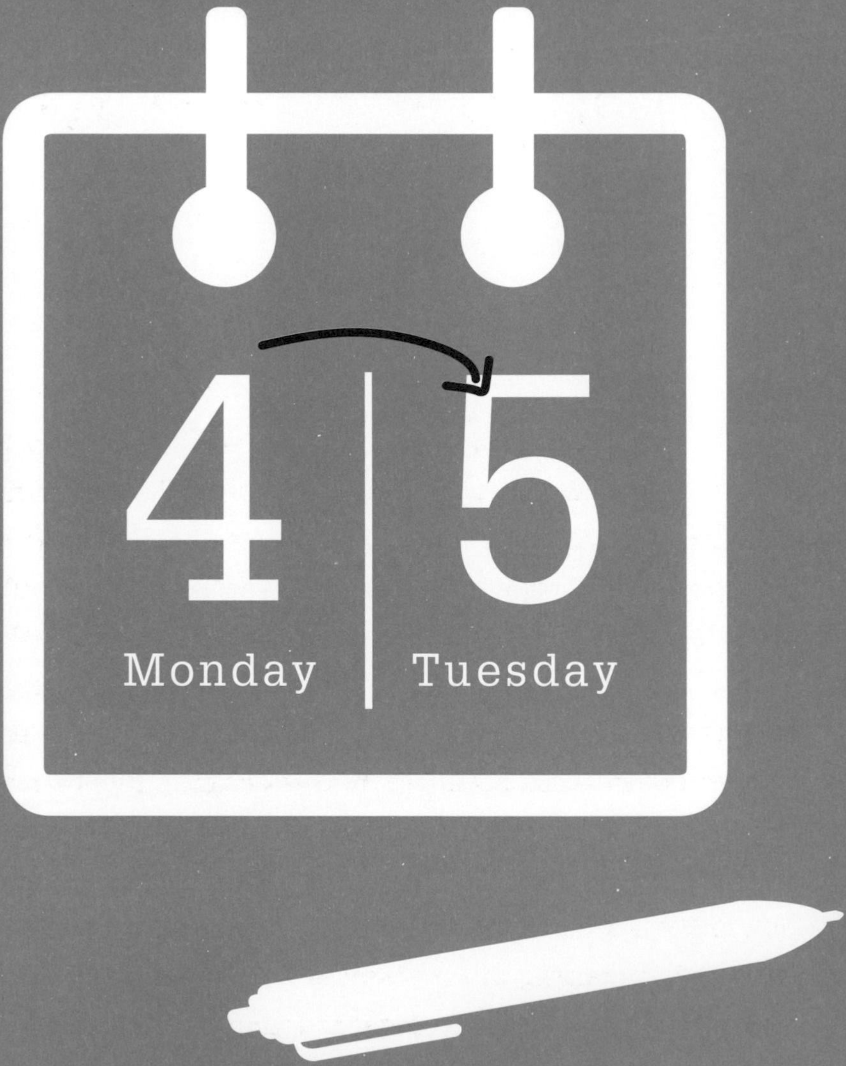
4
5
Monday
Tuesday

Here Today, ~~Gone,~~ ^still Here Tomorrow

There is nothing revolutionary about this style of cooking organisation. My mum was a master at cooking something and then making it stretch out over more than one meal. Our freezer was full of basic meat and tomato sauce, which she would turn into anything from a Bolognese to a chilli con carne. This was the inspiration for my cheats' lasagne and my take on a classic shepherd's pie, using a cobbler topping instead of mashed potatoes. In this chapter, I've taken the idea a step further, throwing in a few of my absolute favourite things to eat: pulled pork, Mexican bean tacos and a very simple Vietnamese noodle salad. I find there's no extra effort involved in making more of something, so this chapter uses the tasty leftovers of one meal to make a different dish the following day or later in the week.

Ham hock with white beans and lemony gremolata

Serves 2 adults and 2 children

1 x 1kg ham hock, preferably smoked (or 800g smoked gammon joint)

1 onion, peeled and halved

2 cloves

1 bay leaf

1 teaspoon peppercorns

For the beans

Olive oil

1 onion, chopped

2 garlic cloves

2 x 400g tins cannellini beans, rinsed and drained

Salt and freshly ground black pepper

For the gremolata

Zest of 1 lemon

1 garlic clove

2 tablespoons chopped flat-leaf parsley

It's odd to think that I only really came to ham hock in the last few years. I don't know why I had not previously been tempted by the wonders of meltingly tender braised meat, from a really good value joint. Pre-cut joints of gammon work very well in this recipe, but if you can get a proper hock of ham (on the bone) it will give you even more flavour and be especially moist. It may seem a bit of a faff to discard the first lot of water, but it will ensure the meat is not too salty. For an extra-sweet flavour, cover the meat with cola instead of water when you slowly braise it. The leftovers can be used to make the ham and pea pasta bake on page 95.

1. Put the ham hock or gammon in a large saucepan and cover it with water. Bring to the boil, allow it to boil for 1 minute then remove from the heat and discard the water.
2. Rinse the ham, return it to the pan and cover again with water (or cola). Add the onion, cloves, bay leaf and peppercorns then bring to the boil. Turn down the heat and simmer for around 2 hours, until the ham is cooked and flaky.
3. Strain the ham, reserving the liquid (**important:** you will need the cooking liquid for the pasta bake the following day, see page 95). Use a knife to pull the ham apart into chunky slices, discarding the skin and bone (if there is one).
4. Heat a glug of olive oil in the saucepan over a medium heat and cook the onion for 4 to 5 minutes before adding the garlic for an extra minute. Mix in the beans and then fill the tin with the reserved ham cooking liquid and add that too. The liquor may still be quite salty, so make sure you taste it at this stage before seasoning with salt and pepper if needed.
5. Add most of the ham hock to the beans (reserving a few handfuls for the pasta bake) and warm through.
6. Chop the lemon zest, garlic and parsley together finely to make the gremolata.
7. Serve the ham and beans and sprinkle over the gremolata.

Ham and pea pasta bake

Next Day

What better way to use up the leftover ham from the ham hock and white beans with gremolata (see page 94) than in a pasta bake? By saving the cooking liquid from the ham and beans the day before, this pasta bake is rich in flavour but by no means heavy. You can, of course, make this dish as a standalone; just replace the cooked ham with store-bought ham and the ham stock with a chicken stock – make sure to season the bake with salt and pepper, as the stock will not have the saltiness of the ham hock stock.

Preheat oven to 180°C/350°F/Gas Mark 4.

1. Cook the pasta according to the packet instructions, then drain it and cool it down with cold water.
2. Meanwhile, heat the butter and olive oil in a saucepan over a medium heat. Add the onion and cook it for a few minutes, until soft, then add the garlic for a further minute.
3. Stir in the flour and cook for 2 minutes, stirring all the time, until it is nutty brown.
4. Pour in the wine, stir quickly to emulsify, then gradually add the ham hock stock until you have a thin sauce – you may not need to use it all. Mix in the crème fraîche, then the mustard and tarragon.
5. Combine the sauce, pasta, peas and ham in your baking dish, sprinkle liberally with cheese and bake for 10 to 15 minutes, until nicely brown on top. Serve immediately with extra freshly grated Parmesan.

Very Easy
★★

Really Quick

Serves 2 adults and 2 children

You will need a 20 x 30cm baking dish

350g penne, rigatoni or other pasta shapes

A big knob of butter

1 tablespoon olive oil

1 onion, finely chopped

2 garlic cloves, crushed

50g plain flour

100ml white wine

500ml reserved ham hock stock

100ml half-fat crème fraîche

2 teaspoons Dijon mustard

1 teaspoon chopped tarragon

200g frozen peas

100g reserved ham hock, cut into small cubes

100g grated cheese (Parmesan or Cheddar), plus extra to serve

One-pot chicken with vegetables

Serves 2 adults and 2 children

Olive oil

Butter

100g smoked bacon, cut into small cubes

2 large carrots, cut into large chunks

200g small new potatoes left whole or halved if large

2 turnips, cut into wedges

1 x 1.5kg chicken

A sprig of tarragon

4 garlic cloves, unpeeled

Salt and freshly ground black pepper

250ml white wine

250ml chicken stock (If you prefer, you can replace part or all of the wine and stock with water)

2 leeks, cut into 2cm slices

50ml single cream (optional)

A squeeze of lemon juice (if using cream)

Everyone loves a traditional roast chicken, but I thought I'd try something a bit different here. Pot-roasting (without an oven in sight) is a great way of cooking a whole chicken, resulting in meat that is always moist and tender. What's more, the veg is cooked with the chicken, so this really is the kind of supper you can put on the heat and say goodbye to, in the knowledge that your whole meal is cooking together nicely. The leftover chicken can then go on to make my delicious Vietnamese salad on page 97.

1. Heat a generous glug of olive oil and a big knob of butter in a casserole or saucepan large enough to hold all the vegetables and the chicken. Fry the bacon until it's just starting to colour, then remove it from the pan and set aside.
2. Add all the vegetables, apart from the leeks, to the pan and cook them until browned. Then remove them and set aside.
3. Finally, brown the chicken on all sides, adding a little more oil and butter if necessary.
4. Leave the chicken breast-side up in the pan, and throw in the bacon, vegetables (not the leeks, yet!), tarragon and garlic. Season with a little salt and pepper, then pour in the wine. Allow the wine to bubble up, before pouring in the stock. The liquid needs to almost cover the chicken, without fully covering the breasts, so top it up with water if you need to. Bring everything to the boil, cover with a lid, lower the heat a little and simmer for about an hour.
5. For the last 10 minutes, add the leeks to the broth.
6. To serve, transfer the chicken and vegetables (except for the garlic cloves) to a large bowl and cover the bowl with foil. Remove the cloves of garlic and when they are cool enough to handle, squeeze the garlic from their skins into the cooking liquid. Boil for 5 minutes to reduce, then stir in the cream and lemon juice, if using.
7. Serve the chicken and vegetables with the gravy.

Vietnamese chicken salad

This minty-sweet fresh salad has become a real favourite in our house – it makes a lovely light supper, but it also sits very nicely in a lunch box. If the title sounds a little exotic, just think of this as a home-made version of the sweet noodle dishes you can buy in the supermarket for lunch. When I serve this for supper, I also make some spring rolls and dip them in the nuoc cham. This is a great way of using up any leftovers from the one-pot chicken on page 96.

1. Cook the noodles according to the packet instructions then drain and cool them completely under cold water.
2. Make the nuoc cham by simply mixing all the ingredients together until the sugar dissolves. Taste the sauce and add a tablespoon of water at a time, until you get a flavour you are happy with – don't make it too runny though.
3. In a large bowl, mix together all the salad ingredients (apart from the nuts) and stir in the sauce.
4. Serve in individual bowls, topped with lots of chopped mint and the chopped peanuts.

Serves 2 adults and 2 children

300g rice noodles

Shredded leftover chicken from the pot roast (approx. 200g)

1 iceberg lettuce, finely shredded

½ cucumber, grated

1 large carrot, grated

A large handful of chopped coriander

A large handful of chopped mint, plus extra to serve

A large handful of plain roasted peanuts, crushed

For the nuoc cham

1 garlic clove, crushed

1 fresh chilli, very finely chopped (choose the chilli according to your heat tolerance. You can also leave it out completely, if you prefer, or add it to individual portions when serving)

Juice of 1 lime

2 tablespoons fish sauce

1 teaspoon sugar

Here Today, Gone, Still Here Tomorrow

Mexican black beans with baked eggs and tortillas

Serves 2 adults and 2 children

Olive oil

2 red onions, finely diced

2 red peppers, deseeded and chopped into 1cm pieces

4 garlic cloves, finely chopped

1 tablespoon ground cumin

1 teaspoon ground coriander

A bunch of coriander, stems finely chopped and leaves left whole

Chipotle paste or sauce, to taste (according to how hot you want it)

400g tin chopped tomatoes

2 x 400g tins black beans, rinsed and drained (or any other type you like, e.g. pinto or red kidney)

A pinch of sugar

Salt and freshly ground black pepper

Juice of 1 lime

1 tablespoon sherry (optional)

4 eggs

4–6 warm tortillas, to serve

I am a huge fan of beans, of all colours and sizes. They are a brilliant, cost-effective way of feeding a family, not to mention that they are full of fine minerals. As a resolute meat-lover, they also never leave me missing the meat. No one knows how to use beans better than the Mexicans and these black beans work superbly both here and in the tacos with black beans, squash and sweetcorn on page 99. Simply save half the beans from this recipe for your tacos later in the week (they will keep well in the fridge for 2 to 3 days). If you think beans can taste bland, I am convinced that these two recipes will change your opinion! If for any reason you are put off by this way of doing the eggs, you can poach or fry them separately.

1. Heat a good glug of olive oil in a large pan, throw in the onions, red peppers and garlic and cook for 2 to 3 minutes – no more. You don't want the vegetables to be soft; this dish needs bite.
2. Add the cumin, ground coriander, the coriander stems and the chipotle paste, stirring to combine everything well.
3. Pour in the tomatoes, 200ml water and the black beans. Finish off with a pinch of sugar, some salt and pepper, the lime juice and the sherry, if you're using it. Simmer for about 10 minutes, until you have a fairly thick sauce.
4. Spoon half the beans into a large frying pan (the reserved beans are for making the tacos on page 99). Make 4 wells in the beans and break an egg into each one. Cook on a medium heat, until the white is set and the yolk is still runny. (Leave it for a little longer if you prefer your yolks set.)
5. Either place the pan in the middle of the table or spoon the beans into separate bowls. Sprinkle with the coriander leaves and serve with warm tortillas for scooping.

Tacos with black beans, squash and sweetcorn

A friend once said to me that cooking butternut squash is a labour of love and I know exactly what she means! Since becoming a dad, I don't have time to spend hours preparing complicated ingredients. So, underneath this recipe I have given you my step-by-step instructions for peeling and cutting butternut squash without any of the faff. I have deliberately not made these tacos spicy but you can easily add some sliced fresh chillies if you want a bit more heat. You will need half the bean quantity from the Mexican black beans on page 98.

Serves 2 adults and 2 children

1 tablespoon olive oil

1 small butternut squash (approx. 500g–600g), cut into 1–2cm cubes

½ x quantity of the black beans on page 98

340g tin sweetcorn, drained

1 pack of taco shells

100ml crème fraîche or sour cream

100g grated Cheddar cheese

For the salsa

1 small red onion, finely diced

1 tomato, deseeded and finely chopped

1 avocado, cut into small cubes

Juice of 1 lime

½ teaspoon cumin

A handful of chopped coriander leaves

1. Put the olive oil in a saucepan on a medium heat, throw in the butternut squash and 100ml water. Cook the squash, partially covered with the lid, until it is nice and soft but not breaking up.
2. Mix in the beans and sweetcorn and continue to heat through for a minute or so.
3. The salsa is quick to make: just combine the red onion, tomato, avocado, lime juice, cumin and coriander leaves in a bowl.
4. To serve, pile a portion of beans in a taco shell, and top with salsa, crème fraîche and cheese.

Note

To peel a butternut squash, put it in the microwave on high for 30 seconds. This softens the skin. Cut a thin slice off the base to make it flat and cut the squash in half at the point where it becomes round. Stand up the straight part of the squash and peel it using a sharp knife, cutting from the top downwards. Do the same with the round base of the squash. To deseed the round base, cut it in half vertically, then cut those two chunks in half. This leaves four nicely shaped chunks with very easy access to the seeds; use a knife to cut away the flesh where the seeds sit.

One-pot pork with cabbage, apples and potatoes

Serves 2 adults and 2 children

A small knob of butter

A small drizzle of olive oil

1 onion, finely chopped

1kg–1.5kg pork shoulder, cut into large chunks

2 garlic cloves, finely chopped

1 teaspoon juniper berries, crushed

1 tablespoon wholegrain or Dijon mustard

1 teaspoon dried oregano

350ml cider or apple juice

350ml water or chicken stock

Salt and freshly ground black pepper

350g baby new potatoes (or cut them to a similar size)

1 small cabbage, cut into wedges

2 eating apples, peeled, cored, cut into eighths

Single cream and crème fraîche, to serve (optional)

Relatively cheap, I find that the flavour of pork marries well with so many spices and aromatics, maybe more so than any other meat. And it can easily hold its own alongside strong flavours. That's why I have added juniper berries to this stew, and also because their sweet aromatic flavour goes so well with the apples. By cooking an extra-large amount of meat, you can enjoy the leftover pork in delicious pulled-pork sandwiches the day after (see page 101). If you own a pressure cooker, the casserole cooking time can be reduced to 30 minutes. If you own a slow cooker, you are looking at 4 to 8 hours, but this is a recipe that works particularly when cooked without rushing.

1. Heat the butter and olive oil in a large casserole on a medium heat. Throw in the onion and cook it for 4 to 5 minutes until soft.
2. Whack up the heat to full and brown the pork all over.
3. Stir in the garlic, juniper berries, mustard and oregano.
4. Pour in your cider or apple juice and the water or stock and season with salt and pepper. Bring the casserole to the boil, then turn down the heat and simmer, covered, for an hour and a half. Keep an eye on it and if the casserole looks like it is drying out at any point, add a little water.
5. Throw in the potatoes and cabbage and cook for a further 20 minutes. Finally, in go the apples; they only need 10 minutes.
6. Serve immediately, with a swirl of cream, if you like. Keep any leftover meat and cooking liquid for the pulled pork on page 101.

Pulled pork in barbecue sauce with coleslaw

After you have made your big vat of pork casserole (see page 100), I guarantee you will have some meaty leftovers. This 'pulled pork' is a totally delicious way of using it up. Pulled pork is traditionally smoked in a smoker or on a barbecue, so it would be ideal if you could get some of that smokiness into the barbecue sauce here. Smoked sweet paprika is the easiest way to achieve this. You could also add a pinch of smoked salt (now widely available in the big supermarkets) or, for full authenticity, a few drops of liquid smoke but, in all honesty, that is a fairly tricky ingredient to get your hands on. Any leftover sauce will keep for about a week in the fridge in an airtight container.

1. First make the barbecue sauce. Heat the oil in a saucepan, add the crushed garlic and fry over a low heat for 1 minute. Stir in the tomato purée and then add all the rest of the ingredients. Simmer for 15 minutes, until the sauce has thickened and reduced – it should coat the back of the spoon. Taste and adjust the seasoning with a little salt and pepper if needed.
2. While the sauce is simmering, make the coleslaw by putting all the vegetables in a large bowl. Mix together the dressing ingredients and coat the vegetables, adding a drop of water if it needs loosening up.
3. Shred the pork using a couple of forks. Put it in a saucepan with the leftover cooking liquid and cook over a high heat until the liquid has evaporated and the pork is starting to crisp up around the edges.
4. Add a couple of tablespoons of the barbecue sauce, stir to coat the pork and continue to crisp the meat a little. You want some of the meat to be quite soft, while the rest is a bit brown and little crunchy.
5. To serve, pile the meat into soft bread baps and top with extra barbecue sauce and the coleslaw.

Serves 2 adults and 2 children

2 or 3 handfuls of leftover pork, along with the cooking liquid
4 soft baps

For the barbecue sauce
Olive oil
2 garlic cloves, crushed
1 tablespoon tomato purée
200g tin chopped tomatoes
1 tablespoon tomato ketchup
1 tablespoon maple syrup
1 tablespoon Dijon mustard
1 tablespoon cider vinegar
1 tablespoon dark brown sugar
½ teaspoon smoked sweet paprika
Salt and freshly ground black pepper

For the coleslaw
1 small white cabbage, cored and finely shredded
2 carrots, grated
½ small onion, finely chopped
50g mayonnaise
50g crème fraîche
½ teaspoon sugar
1 teaspoon cider vinegar
A squeeze of lemon juice
Salt and freshly ground black pepper

Cottage pie with cheese cobbler topping

Serves 2 adults and 2 children

You will need a 20 x 30cm baking dish

For the cottage pie filling
Olive oil
1 onion, finely chopped
1 carrot, finely chopped
1 stick of celery, finely chopped
500g beef mince or leftover cooked roast beef, finely chopped
A few sprigs of thyme, rosemary or flat-leaf parsley
150–200ml red wine
A good squirt of tomato ketchup
2 teaspoons brown sauce (I like good old HP sauce)
Salt and freshly ground black pepper

How do you give a fresh spin on something as traditional as a cottage pie? I am not reinventing any wheels here, but I absolutely love the cobbler topping on this pie! It is not as heavy as dumplings – think of it more like a scone dough. I think that a ragù or Bolognese-style sauce tastes great in a roll so, with this bready topping, you get the best of both worlds. What's more, it makes it much easier to eat the leftovers for lunch the next day – and you don't even need to heat them through again (although you can if you want to). To economise on the meat, you can replace some of it with cooked brown lentils – they will make the sauce lovely and creamy as well. And if you prefer a shepherd's pie, follow the same recipe but just replace the beef with lamb. Make a double batch of this ragù and you can use the rest of it in my cheat's beef lasagne on page 104.

1. Heat a glug of olive oil in a large casserole on a medium heat and cook the vegetables for a few minutes, until softened.
2. Turn up the heat, add the meat and fry it, breaking it up with your spoon, until browned all over. (For extra flavour – although a slightly longer cooking time – cook the meat first in a hot pan with a little oil, without breaking it up, until it has browned on its base. Remove it from the pan and cook the vegetables, and then return the beef to the pan to carry on cooking.)
3. Add the herbs, pour over the wine and allow it to bubble up and reduce a little. Squirt in the tomato ketchup and stir in the brown sauce. Season with salt and pepper.
4. Add a splash of water and simmer for around 20 minutes until the sauce has thickened – you don't want it too loose. If it looks as though it's drying out, add a little more water. Preheat your oven to 200°C/400°F/Gas Mark 6.

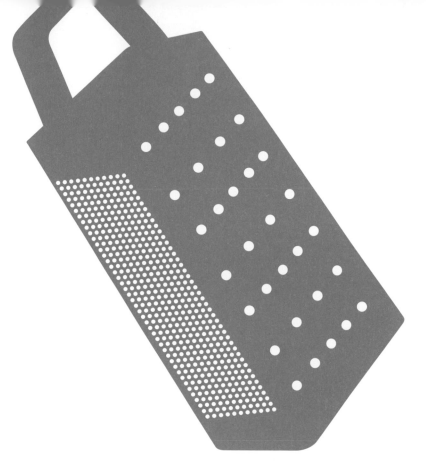

5. While the ragù is simmering, you can make the cobbler topping. Rub together the flour, butter and herbs (if using) and a pinch of salt in a large bowl. Add the cheese and the egg and drizzle in enough milk to make a soft, non-sticky dough. Use your hands to combine the ingredients. Either form the dough into flattish balls, or roll it out to a thickness of about 5mm and cut into rounds of a similar size to small scones.

6. To assemble the dish, spoon the meat mixture into your baking dish and top with the cobbler rounds. Brush the cobbler with the beaten egg and sprinkle with the extra cheese.

7. Bake in the oven for 30 to 35 minutes, until the topping is cooked through and nicely browned.

8. Serve immediately with green vegetables.

For the cobbler topping
200g self-raising flour
50g butter
A pinch of dried oregano or sage (optional)
75g grated Cheddar or other hard cheese
1 large egg
A pinch of salt
Milk, to combine

To finish
1 egg, beaten
Extra grated cheese

Cheat's beef lasagne

Serves 2 adults and 2 children

You will need a 20 x 30cm baking dish

Olive oil

3 garlic cloves, finely chopped

1 x quantity of beef ragù from the cottage pie on page 102

400g tin chopped tomatoes

1 packet of dried lasagne sheets

250g pot of mascarpone cheese

3 x 125g balls of mozzarella cheese, roughly torn

A large handful of basil

Freshly grated Parmesan or Cheddar cheese, for the topping, plus extra

By making a big batch of the ragù for the cottage pie on page 102, this lasagne can be put together in double-quick time, especially as you don't need to make a Béchamel sauce. Instead, the creaminess comes from a pot of mascarpone and some mozzarella cheese – and I actually prefer the taste and consistency of this compared to the traditional method. A final quick tip with lasagne (learned from bitter experience some time ago): never overlap the lasagne sheets. Even though it may look harmless, the double-layered edges simply won't cook!

Preheat the oven to 190°C/375°F/Gas Mark 5.

1. Heat a glug of olive oil in a large saucepan on a low to medium heat. Soften the garlic in the pan for a minute, then pour in the ragù and the tinned tomatoes. Simmer for about 10 minutes, until the tomatoes are cooked and the sauce has slightly reduced.

2. To assemble, spoon one-third of the ragù into your baking dish and smooth it out to form an even layer. Top with a layer of lasagne and one-third of the mascarpone and mozzarella cheeses. Scatter over the basil leaves and then follow with half of the remaining ragù. Top with another layer of lasagne sheets and then cover with half of the remaining cheeses. Spoon over the rest of the ragù and finish with a final layer of lasagne and the rest of the cheeses.

3. Bake in the oven for 35 to 40 minutes until brown and bubbling. Serve immediately.

For a lamb alternative

Instead of using the pre-made ragù, fry a chopped onion
for 4 to 5 minutes, then add 2 crushed garlic cloves
followed by 500g lamb mince. Cook the lamb mince until
browned all over, then stir in 1 teaspoon of crushed fennel
seeds and 1 teaspoon chopped rosemary. Add a 400g tin
of chopped tomatoes, a lamb stock cube and a little extra
water, if necessary. Simmer to make a lovely thick tomato
sauce and then assemble the lasagne, as above.

Inspired Lunch Boxes

We all know that eating a proper meal at lunchtime is the key to ensuring children get enough good stuff into them to last the final part of the school day and to fuel their brains until home time. I can also say that lunch box inspiration is one of the most frequently asked questions I get from parents who get in touch with me. Not that there is anything wrong with a cheese sandwich every so often, but these lunch box ideas take the packed lunch to some refreshingly different places. Needless to say, all of these dishes work well as lunches at home in their own right, too.

Tandoori chicken drumsticks with mint raita

Makes 10–12 pieces

1 pack of chicken
drumsticks (about 1kg)

Salt and freshly ground
black pepper

Juice of 1 lemon,
plus lemon wedges to serve

300ml plain yoghurt

2 teaspoons paprika

2 teaspoons ground
coriander

2 teaspoons ground cumin

½ teaspoon chilli powder
or cayenne pepper

6 garlic cloves, crushed

A small cube of fresh
ginger, grated

For the raita

100ml plain yoghurt

1 tablespoon dried mint
(or chopped fresh mint)

A pinch of sugar

Salt and freshly ground
black pepper

One of my friends, Emma, told me that this recipe
went down a storm at her daughter's netball camp.
Apparently, it was even better than Emma's friend's
mum's jerk chicken, which, up to that point, was the
favourite among the girls! High praise indeed for
these deliciously simple lunchtime treats. You can
buy a readymade tandoori paste but when it's this
easy to make one, why would you? These drumsticks
will turn a golden yellow when grilled. If you want
them to be red, like restaurant tandoori chicken, you
will need to add some red food colouring, which is
not included in the recipe. If you are really stuck for
time and cannot marinate the drumsticks, simply
chuck them in a bowl with the lemon juice, yoghurt
and spices for 10 minutes before grilling. You will
lose some of the depth of flavour but they will still be
much tastier than if you grilled them plain.

1. You will need to remove the skin from the chicken
   drumsticks. This is easily done. The key is to use a
   piece of kitchen paper for extra grip when pulling off
   the skin, starting at the meaty end of the drumstick.
   Keep pulling and give it a good tug to get it off the
   bottom of the drumstick.
2. Slash the drumsticks all over with a sharp knife, put
   them in a bowl, season with salt and pepper and
   cover in the lemon juice. Leave in the fridge for 30 to
   60 minutes.
3. Mix the yoghurt with all the spices, the garlic and the
   ginger. Pour this over the chicken and mix to coat.
   Leave it in the fridge to marinate, preferably overnight
   but for at least a few hours.

4. When you are ready to cook the chicken, preheat your
   grill to high and line your grill pan with foil. Lift the
   chicken out of the marinade and discard any marinade
   still in the bowl – the chicken should be lightly coated
   in the yoghurt but not dripping in it. Grill the chicken
   pieces for 20 minutes, turning regularly, until the chicken
   is cooked through and blackened in places. You can test
   the chicken is cooked by cutting into the fleshy part
   with a sharp knife; there shouldn't be any pink meat.
   You can also bake the chicken in an oven preheated to
   200°C/400°F/Gas Mark 6 for 30 minutes.
5. Make the raita by simply mixing together the ingredients.
   Serve the chicken with the raita and lemon wedges to
   squeeze over the top.

Tuna, carrot and courgette salad

**Makes enough for
4 lunch boxes**

Olive oil

2 carrots, cut into
5mm cubes

2 courgettes, cut into
5mm cubes

160–180g tin tuna, drained

A large handful of finely
chopped flat-leaf parsley

1 orange, cut into segments
(see below)

A few crumbled nuts
(I like walnuts but any
nuts work well)

Fresh mint, to serve

For the dressing

2 tablespoons plain yoghurt

1 garlic clove, crushed

A pinch of curry powder

A pinch of sugar or ½
teaspoon honey

Juice of ½ lemon

1 teaspoon walnut,
hazelnut or olive oil

Salt and freshly ground
black pepper

This is a lovely little salad for a lunch box. It is full of
good stuff and rich in gentle flavours – and it's ideal
for a summer barbecue too. If you want it to go further,
serve it with some lettuce leaves or noodles tossed in
a little oil.

1. Heat a good drizzle of olive oil in a pan on a medium
   heat. Fry the carrots for 3 minutes then add the
   courgettes. Continue cooking until they have softened
   slightly but still have a good firm bite, then transfer them
   to a bowl.
2. Flake over the tuna and stir in the chopped parsley and
   orange segments.
3. Mix together the dressing ingredients, adding the nut
   oil if you have any, or a little olive oil if you don't. If the
   dressing seems very thick, you can thin it slightly with a
   little water.
4. Pour the dressing over the salad and toss well together.
5. Serve with a few crumbled nuts on top and some
   chopped fresh mint.

**To remove the orange segments from
the pithy membrane**

1. Cut a small chunk off the top and bottom of the orange.
   Stand it on a chopping board and peel it by gently
   slicing downwards using a sharp knife or a knife with a
   serrated edge. Then cut the orange segments away from
   the pith. This is easily done by sliding the knife into one
   of the segments, just inside the pith membrane. From
   the bottom of the segment, you can then almost peel
   the orange away from the pith on the other side of the
   segment using your knife. Repeat for the whole orange.

Smoked mackerel and potato salad

My daughter, Matilda, loves smoked mackerel and one of our fallback lunches is smoked mackerel pâté. She is also very fond of potatoes, so I created this salad so she can enjoy the best of both worlds. Think of it as a potato salad with some extra depth of flavour. Mackerel is also one of the healthiest options around, making this a great choice for your children. From a taste standpoint, some cooked beetroot would also go very well in this salad, as long as you don't mind it creating a rather fetching pink dressing.

1. Cook the potatoes in a saucepan of boiling salted water until tender, then drain and cool them slightly under cold running water.
2. Flake the mackerel into small pieces. Cut the potatoes into chunks, and mix them with the mackerel and the spring onions in a bowl.
3. Simply mix together all the dressing ingredients and spoon over the salad. Toss gently and serve. This will keep well in the fridge for a couple of days.

Makes enough for 4 lunch boxes

300g small new potatoes
2 fillets of cold smoked mackerel
4 spring onions, finely sliced

For the dressing
3 tablespoons crème fraîche
1 teaspoon Dijon mustard
1 teaspoon white wine vinegar
A pinch of sugar
Chopped herbs (flat-leaf parsley or dill are great choices)

Feta, cucumber and watermelon salad

Makes enough for 4 lunch boxes

½ cucumber, peeled and cut into 1cm chunks

1 tablespoon white wine vinegar

1 teaspoon sugar

200g feta, cubed

A thick and chunky slice of watermelon, deseeded and cut into chunks (you are looking for a slice roughly the size of a quarter of a small watermelon)

A small handful of chopped mint

Olive oil

Freshly ground black pepper

Juice of ½ lime

I love the mix of flavours in this salad: the saltiness of the feta (one of my favourite fridge standby ingredients), the sweetness of the watermelon and the slight tartness of the dressing. As with all the salads in this chapter, you needn't limit this to lunch boxes; you can easily serve it as a starter or an accompaniment to a summer supper. And try it with the slush on page 180 to use up more of the watermelon!

1. Chuck the cucumber in a bowl, pour over the vinegar and the sugar and toss it all together, making sure the sugar dissolves.
2. Add the feta, cucumber and watermelon and mix well.
3. Stir in the mint, then pour over a little drizzle of olive oil.
4. Season with black pepper (no need for salt, as the feta is salty enough) and finish with a squeeze of lime juice.

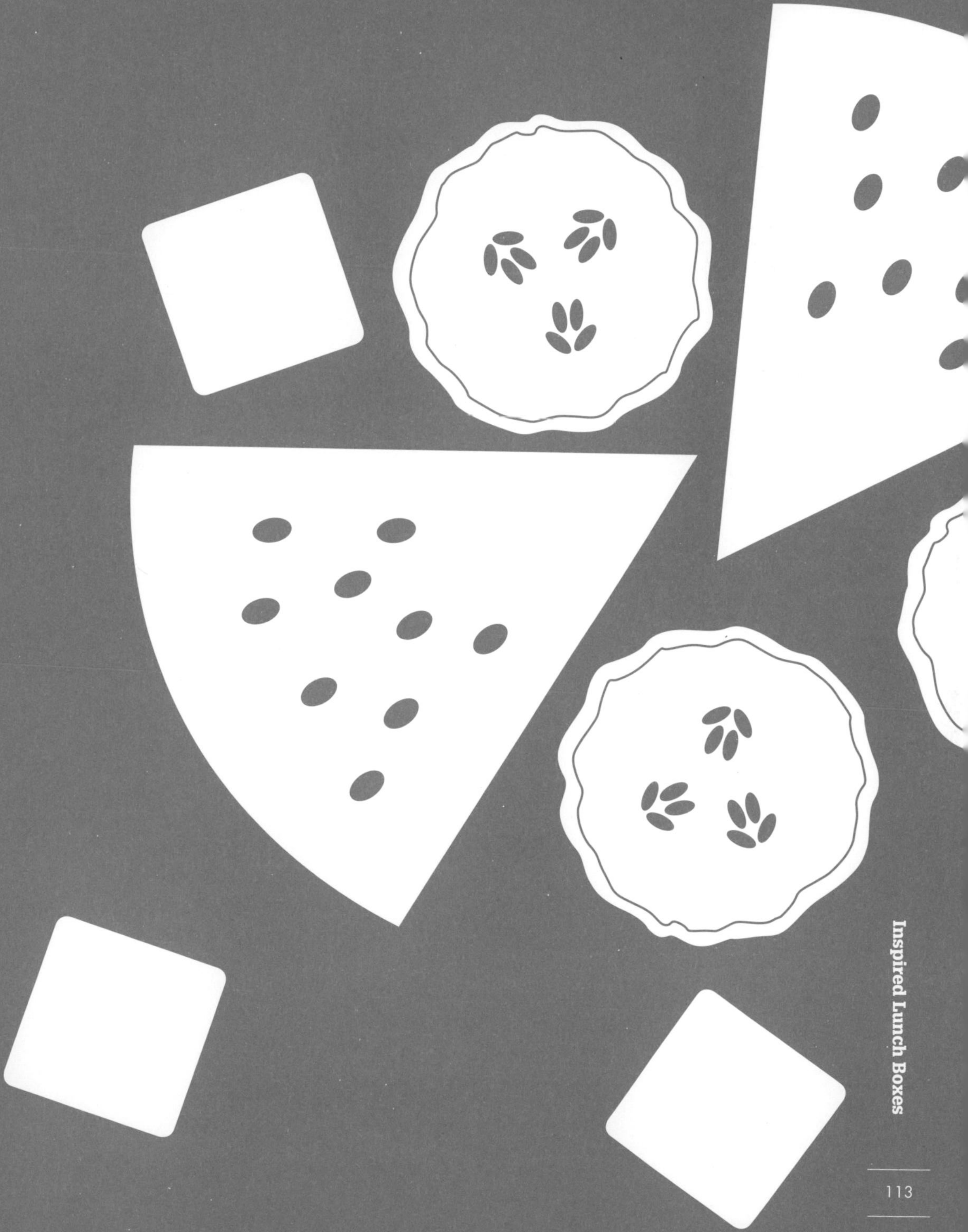

Pittas stuffed with home-made falafel

Makes 4 large pittas

For the falafel

250g chickpeas, soaked overnight with a pinch of bicarbonate of soda (or 400g tinned chickpeas, rinsed and drained)

1 tablespoon ground cumin

1 teaspoon ground coriander

¼ teaspoon ground cinnamon

2 garlic cloves, chopped

3 tablespoons chopped herbs (preferably a mixture of mint, coriander and flat-leaf parsley)

1 tablespoon plain flour

½ teaspoon baking powder

Salt and freshly ground black pepper

Vegetable oil, for frying

One day, supermarkets will sell falafel just like the falafel you get in Middle Eastern restaurants: nice and crispy on the outside and deliciously moist and soft inside. In the meantime, I find making falafel at home a lot of fun. This is the traditional method, using raw, soaked chickpeas. The result is classic falafel, which has a lovely texture and a subtle and delicate balance of flavours. You can use tinned chickpeas if you prefer but the resulting falafel will be slightly softer.

1. Drain the soaked chickpeas and rinse them thoroughly under cold running water.
2. Put all the falafel ingredients in a food processor and blitz until finely chopped but not completely smooth. Chill in the fridge for at least half an hour.
3. Shape about a tablespoon of the chickpea mixture into small, slightly flattened patties.
4. Pour the vegetable oil into a wide, shallow frying pan to a depth of around 5mm. Heat the oil and fry the falafel patties on a medium to high heat until golden on each side – try to turn them only once. Drain on kitchen paper.
5. To make the sauce, mix all the ingredients together and season, to taste, with salt and pepper.
6. To assemble, lightly toast the pitta breads and split into pockets. Fill the pittas with salad of your choice, then add the falafel and drizzle over the sauce. I like to add some chilli sauce to my own pitta.

Note
You can just as easily serve this with the minty raita from the tandoori drumstick recipe on page 108.

For the sauce
100ml tahini
Juice of 1 lemon
2 garlic cloves, crushed
A pinch of cayenne pepper
Salt and freshly ground
black pepper

To serve
1 pitta per person
Chopped lettuce, tomato
and cucumber
Lemon wedges
Freshly chopped coriander,
flat-leaf parsley or mint
Chilli sauce

Dips with a twist

I obviously couldn't do a lunch box section without a few dips. But you wouldn't have let me get away with traditional hummus or a simple tzatziki. So I have taken these two classics and given them a bit of a makeover. In the case of the tzatziki, a reddish-pink makeover, and for the hummus, I have gone green. I particularly like using beetroot, because I feel it is a slightly misunderstood and underappreciated vegetable. Said to reduce fatigue and rich in loads of good-stuff minerals and vitamins, it's the kind of vegetable I want my growing children to eat more of. Serve these dips with sticks of carrot, courgette or cucumber, raw florets of cauliflower, blanched asparagus or green beans and sliced pitta bread. They are also very good on the side with meatballs (see page 144), falafel (see page 114) or some simply grilled fish.

These make enough for 2–4 lunch boxes

Beetroot tzatziki

¼ large cucumber, peeled and finely grated

2 raw beetroots, peeled and finely grated

150ml Greek yoghurt

1 teaspoon Dijon mustard

A squeeze of orange juice

A handful of freshly chopped herbs (dill, tarragon and flat-leaf parsley all work well here)

Salt and freshly ground black pepper

1. Remove as much water as you can from the grated cucumber. You can do this by putting it in a tea towel and wringing it out or by simply giving it a good squeeze in the palm of your hand over the sink.
2. Put all the ingredients in a bowl and mix thoroughly. Taste and adjust the seasoning with salt and pepper and serve chilled.

Pea and feta hummus

Be careful about adding any extra salt
to this one, as the feta is generally salty
enough – taste first.

1. Cook the peas for a couple of minutes in boiling
   water.
2. Drain the peas and put them in a food processor
   along with the rest of the ingredients, including
   a good glug of olive oil for starters. Blitz until
   smooth, drizzling in some extra oil if needed to
   get the right consistency.
3. Serve with a little extra feta crumbled on top.

250g frozen peas

60g feta, crumbled, plus a
little more to garnish

2 tablespoons chopped
fresh mint (or 3 teaspoons
dried mint)

A good squeeze of
lemon juice

Freshly ground black pepper

Olive oil

Sichuan chicken with mangetout and spring onions

Makes enough for 4 lunch boxes

100g mangetout, topped and tailed and sliced diagonally

2 good handfuls of leftover cooked chicken

3 spring onions, sliced diagonally

Freshly ground black pepper

1 teaspoon sesame seeds

For the dressing

2 tablespoons soy sauce

1 teaspoon rice wine vinegar or cider vinegar

1 teaspoon sugar

1 teaspoon finely chopped fresh ginger

1 garlic clove, finely chopped

½ teaspoon ground Sichuan peppercorns

1 tablespoon water or chicken stock

1 teaspoon sesame oil

Freshly ground black pepper

This is a lovely nibbly salad, and a neat way of using up leftover cooked chicken, although you can very easily make it from scratch. Cook a couple of chicken breasts in a bowl (with a little water) in the microwave for around 10 minutes on medium power, or poach them in gently simmering water for 10 minutes, before taking the pan off the heat and leaving the breasts to continue cooking in the water for 15 to 20 minutes. It is definitely worth seeking out Sichuan peppercorns in the big spice collections in larger supermarkets. It's hard to describe their flavour compared with black peppercorns, but they are less hot and, well, a little more tingly!

1. Boil some water in a saucepan, add a pinch of salt and then blanch the mangetout for a couple of minutes. Drain them and then refresh them in cold water.
2. Put the chicken in a serving bowl with the mangetout and spring onions.
3. Mix together all the ingredients for the dressing and pour it over the salad. Mix to combine, then season with black pepper and sprinkle with the sesame seeds.

Lentils with smoked sausage, courgettes and tomatoes

If there's one thing my children love more than sausages, it is a processed Frankfurter-style sausage! I'm more than OK with this and a good old-fashioned hotdog in a roll is a frequent weekend treat at home. However, this delicious cold salad brings the humble Frankfurter slightly more upmarket, as it is served with wholesome lentils and a sweet dressing. You can, of course, cook your own lentils but, for speed and ease, I can't deny that pre-cooked lentils happily find their way into my shopping basket. I am lucky enough to have a wonderful Polish deli near my work and their kielbasa sausages work really well here, too. There's also no reason not to use chorizo, but make sure you fry it separately and drain it fully, as the oil which comes out of it will set once all the ingredients cool down.

Makes enough for 4 lunch boxes

250g cooked lentils (Puy, green or brown) or 100g dried lentils

Olive oil

1 small red onion, sliced lengthways and cut into thin wedges

4 smoked sausages, cut into chunks

1 small courgette, cut into 1cm cubes

4 tomatoes, diced

A handful of torn basil

For the dressing

1 teaspoon mustard (I like Dijon)

1 teaspoon honey

1 teaspoon balsamic vinegar

Olive oil

Salt and freshly ground black pepper

1. If you haven't bought pre-cooked lentils, cook them according the packet instructions. Drain well, tip them into a bowl and leave them to cool a little.
2. Meanwhile, drizzle some olive oil into a frying pan on a medium heat and cook the onion for 2 to 3 minutes, until just softened.
3. Push the onion to one side of the pan and chuck in the sausage and courgette pieces, frying them until they both start browning around the edges and the sausages are hot through.
4. Mix the onion, sausages and courgette with the lentils.
5. Make the dressing by combining the mustard, honey and balsamic vinegar with a glug of olive oil and a splash of water. Season with salt and pepper.
6. Pour the dressing over the lentils, and mix in the tomatoes and torn basil. You can serve this salad while it is still warm, but it is best left to chill completely in the fridge.

Inspired Lunch Boxes

Sweet potato, pea and feta frittata

This frittata could have fitted into almost any of the chapters in this book. Having a good basic frittata in your repertoire will stand you in great stead. I have chucked sweet potato, mint and feta into this recipe but you can use pretty well whatever you want. Most cheeses are great (Cheddar, Parmesan and ricotta, in particular) and any mixture of root vegetables and green vegetables will be lovely. As such, frittatas are a great way of using up any leftover vegetables you may have lurking in the bottom of your fridge.

Makes 8 portions

1 small sweet potato, peeled and cut into cubes

4 eggs

1 teaspoon dried mint (or 1 tablespoon chopped fresh mint)

A pinch of cayenne pepper

Salt and freshly ground black pepper

Olive oil

Butter

100g frozen peas (no need to defrost them)

100g feta, cut into chunks

1. Cook the sweet potato in boiling salted water for 5 minutes, then drain it.
2. Beat the eggs in a bowl and mix in the mint and cayenne pepper. Season with salt and pepper.
3. Heat a really good drizzle of olive oil and a big knob of butter in an omelette pan or frying pan on a medium heat.
4. Evenly arrange the sweet potato and peas over the base of the frying pan, then immediately pour in the eggs. Dot with the cubes of feta. Heat the grill to its highest setting.
5. Cook the frittata until it starts to set and brown around the edges (this will take around 8 minutes), then put the pan under the hot grill for 2 to 3 minutes, until the frittata is slightly puffed and browning. If your frying pan does not have an ovenproof handle, make sure you don't put it directly under the grill.
6. Slide the frittata on to a plate. You can serve it hot, cool or chilled from the fridge.

Prawn, bean sprout and peanut noodle salad

Don't be put off by what may seem like a slightly longer ingredients list than elsewhere in the book. The dressing is very much a store cupboard 'throw-together', and it is also very forgiving. A bit extra, a bit less, a missing ingredient: it will still be delicious.

1. Cook the noodles according to the packet instructions and refresh in iced water. Drain, toss in the oil, then put the noodles in a bowl with the bean sprouts, carrot, cucumber and red pepper.
2. Toss the prawns in the lime juice, season with salt and pepper and add to the noodles and vegetables.
3. Mix together all the dressing ingredients (if you need to, you can loosen it with a little water, a bit more soy sauce or lime juice or some more coconut milk, if you have some to hand.)
4. Pour over the noodle salad and mix gently (hands work best), until everything is well coated. Garnish with coriander leaves, crushed peanuts and lime wedges.

Makes enough for 4 lunch boxes

2 fine egg noodles nests

1 teaspoon sesame or vegetable oil

A handful of bean sprouts

1 carrot, finely cut into strips or grated

¼ large cucumber, cut into small cubes

½ red pepper, deseeded and cut into thin strips

250g cooked prawns

Juice of ½ a lime

Salt and freshly ground black pepper

Coriander leaves

A small handful of peanuts, crushed

Lime wedges, to serve

For the dressing

3 tablespoons peanut butter

1 teaspoon brown sugar or honey

1 teaspoon soy sauce

1 teaspoon fish sauce

Juice of ½ a lime

1 garlic clove, crushed

1cm cube of fresh ginger, finely grated

Chilli sauce or powder, to taste

A little grating of creamed coconut (or you can use 2 tablespoons of coconut milk if you have a tin already open)

Soy and honey glazed salmon with soba noodles

**Makes enough for
4 lunch boxes**

4 x 150g salmon fillets,
skin removed

Olive oil

250g soba noodles

150g Tenderstem broccoli

2 teaspoons sesame oil

3 spring onions, sliced
into rounds

1 teaspoon sesame seeds

For the marinade/dressing

4 tablespoons soy sauce

2 tablespoons honey

½ teaspoon ground ginger

1 garlic clove, crushed

1 tablespoon mirin or rice
wine or a little dash of
sweet sherry (if you can't
find any of these, don't
worry)

1 teaspoon rice wine
vinegar or cider vinegar

Soba noodles (made from buckwheat) are particularly good eaten cold. That's why they are such a perfect fit for this chapter. If you can't find soba noodles (although most big supermarkets do stock them), any other noodles will work well here. Not only is this a lovely addition to a lunch box, it is also exactly the kind of thing I take on a picnic. Oh, and it goes without saying that this dish can just as happily be eaten warm out of the pan.

1. Mix the marinade ingredients together, stirring to make sure the honey is completely incorporated.

2. Place the salmon in a shallow dish and pour the marinade over the top, then leave it in the fridge for as long as you can – at least half an hour, but overnight would be ideal.

3. When you're ready to cook the salmon, heat a little oil in a large frying pan on a medium to high heat. Drain the salmon fillets, reserving the marinade, and fry them for 2 to 3 minutes on each side, until just cooked. It's good to leave the salmon slightly pink in the middle so that it doesn't dry out, plus the salmon will carry on cooking a little when you take it out of the pan.

4. Meanwhile, cook the soba noodles according to the packet instructions and steam or blanch the broccoli for 2 to 3 minutes. Drain and refresh the noodles in ice-cold water, then toss them in the sesame oil.

5. Cut up the cooked broccoli into bite-sized pieces and toss with the noodles and spring onions, then place the salmon on top. If you prefer, you can also flake the salmon into the noodles.

6. Put the frying pan back on the heat and pour in the saved marinade, swirling it around for a few moments to deglaze the pan.

7. Finally, pour the warm marinade over the salmon and noodles, and sprinkle over the sesame seeds.

Rice pilaf with chicken, apple and pine nuts

Perfectly cooked basmati rice in a very gently spiced pilaf, with a little extra sweetness and crunch thanks to the diced apple and grated carrot. You can serve this warm, but I like it as a cold crispy salad. If you have some leftover chicken, chuck it into the rice at the very end of the cooking process, rather than using fresh chicken breasts and cooking them in the stock (but make sure your leftover chicken is properly reheated). Using leftover chicken will also help stop the pilaf becoming too wet.

Makes enough for 4 lunch boxes

Vegetable oil

1 onion, finely chopped

2 garlic cloves, finely chopped

2.5cm cube of fresh ginger, grated

1 teaspoon turmeric

1 teaspoon curry powder

½ stick of cinnamon

2 bay leaves

250g basmati rice, rinsed well

650ml chicken stock or water

Salt and freshly ground black pepper

2 chicken breasts, skin removed and cut into cubes (see intro)

1 apple, peeled and cut into small cubes

Juice of ½ lime

1 large carrot, grated

25g pine nuts, lightly toasted in a dry frying pan

The raita from page 108, to serve

1. Heat a drizzle of vegetable oil in a large saucepan. Add the onion and cook for 4 to 5 minutes, until soft. Add the garlic, ginger and spices and fry for a further minute.
2. Stir in the rice and coat it well in the spices and oil.
3. Pour in the stock and season with salt and pepper. Bring everything to the boil, then turn down the heat to a low simmer and cover the saucepan. Cook for 10 minutes, then carefully mix in the chicken pieces. Try not to stir the rice or it will become creamy, like a risotto.
4. Cover again and cook for 10 minutes, until all the water has evaporated. Keep an eye on it so it doesn't burn or stick to the bottom and make sure the heat isn't too high.
5. Take the pan off the heat and, with the lid still on, leave it to steam for a further 5 to 10 minutes until the rice is soft and fluffy.
6. Just before serving, toss the apple pieces in lime juice and stir them into the rice with the carrot and pine nuts. Serve with the raita.

Ready-Made Meals Made by You

I am not saying we never eat ready-made meals at home. Far from it. But what with the ever-rising cost of our weekly shop, there are times when I wonder whether I can really justify having certain things in our shopping basket. That is why I enjoy trying to replicate – and better – the kind of pre-packaged food you find in the supermarket. None of these dishes will beat a two-minute ping-and-ding microwave operation, but they will give you all the pleasure of home-cooked food compared with mass-produced plastic packs. I decided to have a little fun with this chapter and have gone a bit retro, featuring crispy pancakes, chicken Kievs and sweet and sour pork. Old ones, but great ones nonetheless!

Bean burger with tomato relish

**Serves 2 adults and
2 children**

400g tin beans (any beans,
around 260–280g drained
weight), rinsed and drained

2 eggs, beaten

1 tablespoon finely chopped
flat-leaf parsley

1 teaspoon finely chopped
thyme

25g freshly grated Parmesan
cheese

1 teaspoon Dijon mustard

Salt and freshly ground
black pepper

A squeeze of lemon juice

50g fresh breadcrumbs

Olive oil, for drizzling

A burger made from solely vegetarian ingredients is
never going to be a true replacement for a traditional
burger. But, with the price of meat forever on the
increase, this makes for a frugal and surprisingly, well,
'meaty' alternative. The tomato relish gets made over
and again in my house, served with all manner of
dishes. Simple and delicious, it's worth the small effort
to make your own rather than buy one in a jar.

Preheat your oven to 190°C/375°F/Gas Mark 5.

1. Mash the beans in a bowl using a fork or a masher. You
    don't want a smooth paste here, so it's best not to use
    your food processor.
2. Mix in all the remaining ingredients (apart from the oil),
    making sure everything is well incorporated and leave
    it to rest for 5 minutes.
3. Divide the mixture into quarters and form each piece
    into a burger shape.
4. Place the burgers on a non-stick baking tray (or a baking
    tray lined with greaseproof paper or foil), drizzle them
    with olive oil and bake for 15 to 20 minutes, turning
    halfway through. They will be golden when they are
    ready.
5. While they are cooking, make the tomato relish. Heat
    a drizzle of oil in a saucepan on a gentle medium heat
    and cook the onion and garlic for 4 to 5 minutes to
    soften them.

6. Chuck in the tomatoes, sugar and vinegar and simmer until the tomatoes are just beginning to break down and have started to reduce. You want it to have a slightly jammy consistency. Stir through the chilli sauce, to taste.

7. Serve the burgers in buns with the relish, grated cheese if you fancy it, and any of your favourite burger toppings.

For the tomato relish

Olive oil

1 small red onion, finely diced

1 garlic clove, crushed (optional)

4 medium tomatoes, deseeded and finely chopped (no need to peel)

½ teaspoon brown sugar

1 teaspoon red wine vinegar

Chilli sauce (such as Tabasco), to taste

To serve

Burger buns

Freshly grated cheese (optional)

Your favourite burger topping, such as lettuce and gherkins

Portobello mushroom burger with escalivada and goat's cheese

Serves 2 adults and 2 children

1 small aubergine, cut into 1–2cm cubes

1 small red pepper, deseeded and thinly sliced

4 tomatoes, quartered

4 garlic cloves, unpeeled

Olive oil

1 teaspoon red wine vinegar

Salt and freshly ground black pepper

4 large portobello or field mushrooms

4 slices of goat's cheese, cut from a log

Rolls or buns, to serve

Portobello mushrooms (or large field mushrooms) are meaty in texture, very filling and fairly cheap to boot. They make a great alternative to the classic burger and are fantastic with all the usual burger toppings – simply grill or bake the mushrooms and then add your favourite extras. I love the Spanish flavours in the escalivada here (a Catalan dish almost like a ratatouille) which elevates these humble mushrooms to a vegetarian spectacular that will satisfy the hungriest of tummies.

Preheat your oven to 180°C/350°F/Gas Mark 4.

1. Put the aubergine, red pepper, tomatoes and garlic in a roasting dish and cover them with a really good glug of olive oil. Roast the vegetables for 30 to 40 minutes (stirring halfway through), until they are soft and starting to turn a little bit golden.

2. Remove the dish from the oven (but keep the oven at the same temperature), squeeze the flesh from the garlic cloves and discard the skins. Mix everything together, stir in the vinegar and season with salt and pepper. Set aside to cool a little.

3. Meanwhile, place the mushrooms in a baking dish. Baste them with a little olive oil, season with salt and pepper and cook them in the oven for 10 minutes.

4. Spoon the escalivada equally between the mushrooms (but don't overfill them) and place the goat's cheese slices on top. Drizzle a little olive oil over the cheese, return them to the oven and cook for 10 minutes, until the cheese has melted and the escalivada is warmed through.

5. Serve the stuffed mushrooms in rolls.

Retro sweet and sour pork

I particularly love the fact that this dish carries all the sweet, tangy punch of a true sweet and sour, without any additives or food colouring. But you won't notice the difference between this version and the classic dish we all enjoy at our local Chinese restaurant. To be fully authentic, I have used a batter for the pork, but if you prefer, you can just dust the pork with cornflour after a quick marinade in the soy sauce and Chinese five spice and then simply fry the meat in a little less oil. You can also use chicken breasts or thighs instead of the pork.

Serves 2 adults and 2 children

300g lean pork, cubed

1 tablespoon soy sauce

1 teaspoon Chinese five spice

Vegetable oil

1 red pepper, deseeded and cut into chunks

1 carrot, thinly sliced on the diagonal

4 spring onions, cut into 1cm rounds

225g tin water chestnuts, drained

225g tin pineapple cubes in own juice (reserve the juice)

Sesame oil (optional)

Cooked plain white rice, to serve

For the pork batter

1 egg, beaten

2 tablespoons cornflour, plus extra for dusting

For the sauce

Reserved pineapple juice

1 tablespoon soy sauce

1 tablespoon rice wine vinegar or cider vinegar

1 tablespoon brown sugar

2 tablespoons tomato purée

1 tablespoon cornflour (optional)

1. First make the sauce. Measure out the pineapple juice and top it up with either water or additional juice until you have 150ml liquid. Mix this together with the rest of the sauce ingredients. If you want the end result to be slightly thickened, as in the traditional takeaway dish, mix the cornflour with a little water and stir it into the mixed ingredients. If you leave out the cornflour, the sauce will be looser. Set the sauce aside.

2. In a small bowl toss the pork in the soy sauce and Chinese five spice.

3. Make the batter by simply mixing together the egg and cornflour in a shallow dish. Drain the pork and coat it in the batter.

4. Pour vegetable oil into a wok to a depth of about 5mm. Heat over a high heat and when almost smoking, carefully drop in the battered pork. Cook the pork, turning it a few times in the oil, until golden. Remove and drain on kitchen paper.

5. Drain off most of the oil from the wok and then put it back on the heat. Fry the vegetables until they are just cooked through, then add the water chestnuts, pineapple and sauce. Bring it to the boil, stirring all the time so it thickens evenly (if you are using the cornflour).

6. Return the pork to the wok and heat through for a couple of minutes. Serve with white rice.

Pad Thai

Serves 2 adults and 2 children

225g flat rice noodles

Vegetable oil

10–12 large raw shelled prawns

50g firm tofu, cut into cubes

2 shallots or 1 small onion, chopped

1 carrot, cut into thin batons or grated

A large handful of mangetout, topped and tailed and cut into thirds, diagonally

2 garlic cloves, chopped

1 egg, beaten

For the sauce

1 tablespoon palm sugar (or light brown sugar)

1 tablespoon granulated or caster sugar

1 tablespoon tamarind paste or purée (Bart does a good one in a jar)

2 tablespoons fish sauce

½ teaspoon shrimp paste (optional)

Salt and freshly ground black pepper

Pad Thai is one of those dishes that has a slightly mystical aura surrounding it. It is actually much easier to make than you think, with its signature taste coming from a few key ingredients. Tamarind paste or purée is now readily available in supermarkets, and it is a great addition to your store cupboard, not least for chucking into curries to add extra depth. It's worth pointing out here that the topping really does finish off this dish. The extra crunch from the peanuts really enhances the deliciousness and creates an authentic Pad Thai experience. If you prefer, you can use chicken instead of prawns and interchange whatever vegetables you have to hand.

1. Heat all the sauce ingredients together in a small saucepan, stirring gently, until the sugar has dissolved. Taste and season with salt and pepper if you feel they are needed. Set the sauce aside.
2. Cook the noodles according to the packet instructions. Drain and refresh them in cold water so that they stop cooking.
3. Heat a little vegetable oil in a wok or large frying pan over a high heat. Fry the prawns briskly, stirring all the time, then remove them as soon as they are pink. Add a little more oil and fry the tofu, keeping it moving, and then set that aside too.
4. Stir-fry the vegetables and when they are just cooked through, add the garlic and fry for a moment more.
5. Push all the vegetables to one side of the pan, pour in the beaten egg and stir until it starts to look a little scrambled. Now mix the egg with the vegetables.

6. Chuck the prawns and tofu back into the wok, along with the noodles. Stir gently but thoroughly to warm the noodles and combine all the ingredients.

7. Pour the sauce over the top and toss together. Serve immediately, sprinkled with the spring onions, coriander and peanuts, and with some lime wedges for squeezing over.

To serve

2 spring onions, shredded

A handful of coriander leaves

2 tablespoons roasted peanuts, lightly crushed

Lime wedges

Crispy pancakes

Serves 2 adults and 2 children

For the pancakes
125g plain flour
Salt
2 eggs
300ml milk
A drizzle of vegetable oil
Butter

For the cheese sauce filling
30g butter
30g plain flour
300ml milk
1 teaspoon Dijon mustard
100g grated cheese (pick one with a nice strong flavour like Cheddar or Gruyère)

Optional extras
Chopped ham
Cooked chicken
Mushrooms fried in butter and garlic
Frozen peas
Sweetcorn

I am diving right into the world of Findus here with these crispy pancakes. Do you remember the adverts back in the 1980s? I think the slogan was 'every day has got a different taste'. I also remember a rather clumsy dad trying very hard to amuse an extremely cute little baby. The beauty of these pancakes is that they really do mean that every day can have a different taste, as the fillings can vary enormously, especially if you have leftovers such as ham and cooked chicken. My children enjoy grabbing things and adding them to their own pancakes before they are cooked, so it's a great way to get them involved. If you can't face making the actual pancakes, you have two options: supermarkets sell good-value packets of readymade pancakes (look out for the smaller pancakes) or you can also use small flour tortillas. These have the advantage of being slightly harder to tear than pancakes.

1. If you are making the pancakes, sift the flour into a bowl, then throw in the salt, eggs and milk. Mix with a whisk until nice and smooth. Stir in a drizzle of vegetable oil.
2. Heat a smallish pancake pan or frying pan on a nice high heat. Melt a small knob butter in the pan, swizzle it around then add a small ladleful of batter, swirling it round the base of the pan. You are not looking for big pancakes here – 10cm in diameter is perfect.
3. When the batter has set (this will be quick – just a few seconds), flip over the pancake and cook it for a further 30 seconds. Remove the cooked pancake and repeat with the rest of the batter. It is fine to stack the pancakes on top of each other while you cook the rest; they will not stick together.

4. To make the cheese sauce, melt the butter in a saucepan on a medium heat then stir in the flour. It is important to mix well and keep stirring for a minute or so. Drop in a splash of milk and stir to combine it into the flour and butter. Gradually add the rest of the milk, stirring or whisking the whole time. You will end up with a fairly thick sauce (like custard). Remove the sauce from the heat and whisk in the mustard and cheese. Keep stirring until it is all melted.

5. To assemble the pancakes, place about 2 tablespoons of sauce in the middle of each pancake, just to one side, and add in any of your optional extra fillings.

6. Make a 'glue' by mixing 1 tablespoon of plain flour with an equal amount of water. Add more water if it is too thick. Brush the edge of each pancake with the flour and water mixture, then fold the pancake over and press it gently so you have a sealed half moon.

7. Put the flour in a shallow dish, the egg in another dish and the breadcrumbs in a third. Carefully dip the pancakes first in the flour (shaking off any excess), then in the egg and, finally, in the breadcrumbs. Make sure they are evenly coated all over.

8. Heat a good glug of vegetable oil in a large frying pan over a medium to high heat. When the oil is hot, fry a pancake for a minute on each side, until it is well browned. Drain on kitchen paper and serve immediately. Repeat for the remaining pancakes, making sure to add more oil each time.

To finish

3–4 tbsp plain flour

1 egg, beaten

A large handful of breadcrumbs

Vegetable oil

Chicken Kievs

Serves 2 adults and 2 children

150g butter, at room temperature

5 garlic cloves, crushed

Salt and freshly ground black pepper

Juice of 1 lemon

A handful of flat-leaf parsley, finely chopped

4 skinless chicken breasts, with small fillet attached

50g plain flour, seasoned with salt and pepper

2 eggs, beaten

100g breadcrumbs

Vegetable oil

Lemon wedges, to serve

There is something wonderfully old-fashioned about chicken Kievs. Maybe it's simply the fact that the whole point of them is to have a load of lovely, flavoursome melted butter dripping out when you cut into them! Still, my Gran always said that a little bit of everything is fine, so I am more than happy to serve these at home once in a while. If the preparation seems quite involved to you, the great thing about these Kievs is that they freeze beautifully before the breadcrumb stage so you can make an extra-large batch and save the ones you don't need for a rainy day. The technique of butterflying the chicken breasts is honestly not as difficult as it sounds and is the perfect way to ensure the chicken is nice and flat for cooking.

1. Mix the butter with the garlic, 1 teaspoon of salt, half a teaspoon of pepper, the lemon juice and parsley. If you have the time, chill it until it is firm again.
2. Now you need to butterfly and flatten the chicken breasts. Remove the small fillet from the back of the chicken breast and place the main chicken breast smooth side down. Cut from the top to the bottom along the centre of the breast, about halfway through the flesh – be careful not to cut all the way through. Now make gentle cuts along the same length, working out towards each edge of the breast until you can open it up and lay it out flat. Don't go too close to the edge or you will cut off the top of the breast.
3. Place each breast between cling film or greaseproof paper and bash it with a rolling pin to flatten slightly and tenderize the meat. Season the breasts with salt and pepper.

4. Drop a quarter of the garlic and butter mixture into the centre of each breast, then place the reserved small fillet on top. Fold the chicken breast back together, overlapping the edges slightly and sealing with a little bit of the egg and flour. If you have time, wrap each chicken breast tightly in cling film and chill for a couple of hours in the fridge. You can also freeze them very successfully at this stage if you want to make a larger batch.

5. When you are ready to cook the Kievs, preheat your oven to 200°C/400°F/Gas Mark 6. Tip the flour into a shallow dish, the beaten eggs into another dish and the breadcrumbs into a third. Roll the chicken breasts first in the flour (shaking off the excess), then dip them in the egg and finally coat them in breadcrumbs. Make sure they are evenly coated all over.

6. Lightly oil a frying pan and place on a medium heat. Fry the Kievs for a couple of minutes on each side, until they are golden brown.

7. Transfer the Kievs to a baking tray and cook in the oven for a further 15 minutes. Serve with the lemon wedges, steamed green beans and mashed potatoes to soak up all the lovely garlicky butter.

Traditional chicken and chorizo paella

Serves 2 adults and 2 children

200g chorizo sausage, cut into small cubes

4–6 chicken thighs (approx. 500g), skin and bone removed, cut into cubes

1 onion, finely chopped

4 garlic cloves, finely chopped

1 teaspoon smoked paprika

100g green beans, trimmed and cut in half

100g broad beans

A pinch of saffron, soaked in a little warm water (or a pinch of turmeric)

1L chicken stock or water

300g paella rice

Salt and freshly ground black pepper

Lemon wedges, to serve

This paella is cooked in the traditional way, on the stovetop, as opposed to being baked in the oven. It is also very meaty, rather than being all about the seafood. The beauty of cooking paella on the hob is that it needs virtually no attention at all. Just get all the ingredients in the pan and leave it be. In fact, I would actively encourage you to leave the base of the paella to crisp up a little (not actually burn, but not far off it!). The Spanish call this caramelized crust the socarrat and it is, in some ways, the best part of the dish – for me, anyway. I don't have the luxury of a proper wide, flat-bottomed paella pan (or the space to cook with it) so your normal frying pan will do the trick here.

1. Heat your frying pan over a medium heat and add the chorizo. Cook it until it is crispy (but do not burn it) and its delicious red oil has been released.
2. Add the chicken and the onion and stir to coat in all the lovely chorizo oil. Cook for 3 to 4 minutes until the chicken has browned. Mix in the garlic and paprika and stir for a few seconds.
3. Add the green beans and broad beans to the pan and give them a good stir. Pour over the saffron (and its soaking water) and the stock. Bring to the boil and simmer for a couple of minutes to help the beans along, then pour in the rice.
4. If the rice isn't completely submerged, add enough water to just cover it. Season with salt and pepper and leave the paella to cook for about 12 minutes, checking occasionally to make sure the top hasn't dried out – add a little more water if needed. You want the rice to be nicely puffed and cooked through.
5. Remove the pan from the heat, cover it with the lid or a clean tea towel and allow the rice to finish cooking in the steam for about 10 minutes.
6. Serve immediately with lemon wedges.

Lamb and potato hotpot

Lamb hotpot is like an old friend: you know exactly what to expect, it's reliable, comforting and never lets you down. I have bulked up my version by adding swede and carrots and this recipe is also slightly quicker to cook than traditional hotpot. The key is to use neck fillet, also called the scruff. It is a good-value cut, widely available and, as it is not from a part of the lamb that does the hard work, it is tender and does not require an extended cooking time. However, there is no reason why you can't use shoulder here, or any other cut of lamb for that matter. Shoulder require an extra 30 minutes of cooking time.

Serves 2 adults and 2 children

500g neck fillet, sliced into rounds

1 tablespoon plain flour

1 teaspoon mustard powder

Salt and freshly ground black pepper

Olive oil

Butter

1 large onion, halved and sliced

2 carrots, cut into large chunks

½ small swede, cut into chunks

1 sprig of thyme

600g potatoes, peeled and fairly thinly sliced (aim for about 3–4mm)

500ml lamb or chicken stock or water

Preheat your oven to 200°C/400°F/Gas Mark 6.

1. Chuck your meat into a bowl. Add the flour, mustard powder, salt and pepper and give it a good stir to make sure the meat is evenly coated.
2. Heat a nice glug of olive oil and a knob of butter in an ovenproof casserole and sear the meat to seal it on all sides. Depending on the size of your casserole, you may need to do this in two quick batches so as not to cram it too full.
3. Remove the meat and set aside while you fry the onion for 4 to 5 minutes until soft.
4. Layer the casserole with half the meat, then half the onion, followed by half of the root vegetables. Repeat these layers and tuck in the sprig of thyme.
5. Finish with slices of potato arranged neatly on top.
6. Carefully pour over the stock, cover the casserole with a lid and cook in the oven for 20 minutes, before turning down the heat to 140°C/275°F/Gas Mark 1. Cook for a further 1 hour and 15 minutes.
7. Remove from the oven and dot the potatoes with small pieces of butter. Turn the oven back up to 200°C/400°F/ Gas Mark 6 and cook the hotpot, uncovered, for a further 5 minutes, allowing the potatoes to turn a lovely golden colour. Serve immediately.

Southern fried chicken with corn on the cob and greens

**Serves 2 adults and
2 children**

8–10 thighs or drumsticks,
or a mixture (approx. 1kg)

284ml pot buttermilk

Salt and freshly ground
black pepper

1 teaspoon onion powder

150g plain flour

½ teaspoon paprika (sweet
or hot, it's up to you)

½ teaspoon mustard powder

½ teaspoon dried oregano
or sage

Vegetable oil

I am making these finger-licking chicken pieces the traditional way, by frying them. If you prefer, you can cook them in the oven. Heat a baking tray with a little oil in an oven preheated to 180˚C/350˚F/Gas Mark 4. Carefully roll the chicken pieces in the hot oil and then bake them for around 30 minutes. Although it may feel like a bit of a faff to marinate the chicken, it really helps tenderise and flavour the meat. That said, I have also made this chicken without marinating it and it was still lovely.

1. Using a sharp knife, cut some slashes into the chicken pieces. Put them in a bowl and cover them with the buttermilk. Season with 1 teaspoon of salt and pepper, and mix in the onion powder. Give it a good rub to work it into the meat, then leave in the fridge to soak for at least a few hours – and ideally overnight. When you are ready to fry the chicken, let it come back to room temperature first.

2. In a bowl, mix the flour with paprika, mustard powder and dried herbs and season with salt and pepper. Wipe the buttermilk from the chicken and coat each piece in the seasoned flour. Shake to remove any excess.

3. Heat a deep-fat fryer to 160°C. If you are using a saucepan, make sure the oil is no more than about one-third of the way up the pan. Test the oil with a small piece of bread – it should immediately bubble furiously and turn brown within about 20 seconds. (You can shallow fry the chicken if you prefer, turning it 3 or 4 times while cooking.)

4. Fry the chicken for 10 to 15 minutes until it is deep golden brown and fully cooked through.

5. While the chicken is cooking, bring a large pan of salted water to the boil and cook the corn cobs for 3 minutes. Drain away the water and allow a good knob of butter to melt over the cob pieces, before seasoning with salt and pepper.

6. Shred the greens, then heat 1 tablespoon of olive oil and a large knob of butter in a wide frying pan. Fry the greens for 2 minutes, before adding the garlic. Cook for another couple of minutes then add a splash of water, cover with a lid and cook the greens until they are soft and just starting to collapse down – about 2 to 3 minutes. Season with salt and pepper and a squeeze of lemon juice just before serving with the chicken and the corn cobs.

For the corn

4 corn on the cob,
each cut into 3 wedges

Butter

Salt and freshly ground
black pepper

For the greens

500g spring greens or green cabbage (don't use spinach, as it breaks down too much. If you are using kale, separate the leaves from the stems)

Olive oil

Butter

1 garlic clove

Salt and freshly ground
black pepper

A squeeze of lemon juice

Salmon fishcakes with dill and mustard mayonnaise

Serves 2 adults and 2 children

400g floury potatoes (e.g. Maris Piper or King Edward), peeled, cut into chunks

Salt and freshly ground black pepper

400g tin salmon

Zest 1 lemon

4–5 tbsp plain flour

1 large egg, beaten

50g breadcrumbs (panko breadcrumbs are my favourite)

Vegetable oil

For the mayonnaise

1 egg yolk

1 teaspoon Dijon mustard

A dash of Tabasco

Salt and freshly ground black pepper

300ml vegetable oil

1 teaspoon lemon juice

A small bunch of dill, chopped

I have deliberately kept these yummy fishcakes very simple, as there is plenty of extra flavour in the mayonnaise. If you can't be bothered to make your own mayonnaise, feel free to use a small jar of store-bought mayonnaise and just add the lemon juice, mustard and lots of dill to that. I have cheated a little by using tinned salmon. It is, of course, cheaper than fresh salmon and, in all honesty, does the job just fine. If you want to use fresh salmon, you'll need a couple of skinless fillets and the easiest way to cook them (ensuring less washing up) is to pop them in the simmering water with the potatoes for the last 5 minutes of cooking time.

1. Put the potatoes in a saucepan, cover them with water and bring to the boil. Leave them to simmer for 10 to 15 minutes until they are soft. Drain them in a colander and then leave them in the colander for a couple of minutes to dry out. Mash them and season.
2. Mix the salmon and the lemon zest into the potatoes.
3. Shape the fishcake mixture into 4 large or 8 small cakes. Dust each one with flour, shaking off the excess. Dip them into the egg and finally coat in the breadcrumbs.
4. Heat a really good glug of oil in a large frying pan and fry the fishcakes for 3 to 4 minutes on each side until they are a deep golden brown and hot in the middle. (You can also bake the fishcakes for 10 minutes in an oven preheated to 180°C/350°F/Gas Mark 4.)
5. If you are making home-made mayonnaise, mix together the egg yolk, mustard, a dash of Tabasco and a little salt, then dribble in a tiny amount of oil, beating well until it starts to emulsify. Once it starts to emulsify, you can drip in the oil a bit faster, until it has all been added. Right at the end, stir in the lemon juice and chopped dill and season with salt and pepper, if necessary.

Spicy sausage pasta bake

This is a huge hit in my house and beyond. As one of my friends said: 'What's not to like about pasta and sausages?!' I couldn't have put it better myself. When I have a little more time, I squeeze the meat from the sausages and roll it into balls, before frying them like meatballs. I really would recommend using good-quality meaty sausages, as they will hold their shape better during cooking. If you can get hold of some spicy Italian sausages from your butcher, deli or supermarket, this dish will be even lovelier. There is not very much cream here so, if you don't have a leftover dollop to use up, you can omit it. That said, it does add something to the bake, giving it a little, well, creamy texture.

You will need a 20 x 30cm baking dish

6–8 large sausages

Olive oil

350g pasta shapes (penne or conchiglie work well here)

100g grated hard cheese (I like to use Parmesan, pecorino or Cheddar)

For the sauce

200ml red wine

A sprig of rosemary

1 x quantity of tomato sauce (from spaghetti and meatballs recipe on page 144)

A pinch of ground cinnamon

1 teaspoon chilli flakes or powder (to taste)

Salt and freshly ground black pepper

50ml double cream

Preheat your oven to 180°C/350°F/Gas Mark 4.

1. Place the sausages in the oven dish you will use for the pasta bake, drizzle them with olive oil and cook them in the oven for 15 to 20 minutes.
2. Meanwhile, cook the pasta in a large pan of salted water according to the packet instructions, then drain in a colander.
3. While the sausages and pasta are cooking, make the sauce. Pour the wine into a saucepan and add the rosemary. Bring to the boil and boil fiercely to reduce by at least half.
4. Add the tomato sauce, cinnamon and chilli, along with 100ml water. Season with salt and pepper, then simmer until the sauce tastes lovely and rich but isn't too thick. Mix in the double cream, if you're using it.
5. When the sauce, pasta and sausages are ready, remove the sausages from the oven, drain away any fat and cut them into rounds.
6. Return the sausages to the oven dish and mix with the sauce and pasta. Sprinkle over the cheese and bake for 20 to 25 minutes. Serve hot from the oven.

Quick chicken curry with pilau rice

Serves 2 adults and 2 children

For the spice blend

1 teaspoon coriander seeds

1 teaspoon cumin seeds

1cm piece of cinnamon stick

2 spokes of star anise

1 cardamom pod

1 bay leaf

1 teaspoon fennel seeds

1 teaspoon black peppercorns

½ teaspoon Nigella seeds

A few gratings of fresh nutmeg

1 teaspoon turmeric

½ teaspoon cayenne pepper or chilli powder, to taste

You may have looked at the ingredients for the spice blend mix and thought, 'Which part of this quick chicken curry is actually quick?!'. Well, if you prefer, you can use your favourite curry powder but I thought it would be a shame not to include a recipe because you can easily make a large quantity of it and store it in a jar. As long as you keep it in a cool dark place (the technical term for this is a cupboard!) it will last a few months. For extra speed, serve the curry with flatbreads, but the pilau rice is rather lovely and goes perfectly.

1. If you are making your own spice mix, put all the whole spices in a dry frying pan and toast them on a medium heat until they give off a lovely aroma – be very careful not to burn them. Remove the spices from the frying pan and tip them on to a plate to cool them down (if you leave them in the frying pan they'll continue to cook). When cool, grind them in a spice grinder or with a pestle and mortar and mix with the rest of the spices.

2. Now make a start on the pilau rice. Heat 2 tablespoons of vegetable oil in a lidded saucepan. Add the spices, cook them for a minute then chuck in the onion.

3. Fry the onion for 2 minutes then mix in the turmeric, rice and sultanas or raisins if you are using them. Stir to combine then add the stock or water and season with salt and pepper.

4. Bring to the boil, then turn down the heat and let it simmer gently. Cover with the lid and leave to cook for 10 to 15 minutes until all the water is absorbed.

5. While the rice is still bubbling away, make the curry. Heat 2 tablespoons of vegetable oil in a large saucepan. Add the onion and cook over a low to medium heat until broken down, soft and a light golden brown. Add the garlic and ginger and cook, stirring for a minute.

6. In go the spices, followed by the tomato purée. Stir to cook the tomato purée for a couple of minutes, then add the tomatoes and a pinch of sugar. Season with salt and pepper and splash in a little water, then cover with the lid and simmer for 5 minutes.

7. The rice should have absorbed all of the water by now, so take the pan off the heat. Remove the lid and place a folded tea towel over the top of the pan and allow the rice to steam for a further 5 minutes or so before serving. (Please make sure you have turned off the gas before leaving the rice to steam. From personal experience, that towel catches fire mighty quickly – and in the ensuing panic, you will ruin the rice too! Trust me.)

8. While the rice is steaming, throw the chicken into the curry, mix well and leave it to simmer for 5 minutes or so, until the chicken is fully cooked through.

9. Stir the yoghurt through the curry and serve with the coriander, chillies (to taste), wedges of lemon and a lovely mound of rice.

For the pilau rice
Vegetable oil
½ teaspoon cumin seeds
½ teaspoon coriander seeds, crushed
1 cardamom pod, seeds only
3cm piece of cinnamon stick
1 bay leaf
1 small onion, finely chopped
½ teaspoon turmeric
250ml basmati rice
50g raisins or sultanas (optional)
650ml chicken stock or water
Salt and freshly ground black pepper

For the curry
Vegetable oil
1 onion, finely sliced
2 garlic cloves, finely chopped
3cm cube of fresh ginger, grated
1 tablespoon spice blend or curry powder (see below)
1 tablespoon tomato purée
100g fresh or tinned chopped tomatoes
A pinch of sugar
Salt and freshly ground black pepper
8 chicken thighs, skin and bone removed, cut into bite-sized pieces
4 tablespoons plain yoghurt

To serve
A handful of coriander leaves
Sliced green chillies (for the adults)
Lemon wedges

Spaghetti with meatballs

Serves 2 adults and 2 children

350g spaghetti
Torn basil and freshly grated Parmesan cheese, to serve

For the sauce
Olive oil
1 onion, finely sliced
2 garlic cloves, crushed
1 teaspoon dried oregano
1 bay leaf
400g tin chopped tomatoes
A pinch of sugar (optional)
Salt and freshly ground black pepper

For the meatballs
250g minced beef
250g minced pork
100g finely chopped smoked bacon
100g fresh breadcrumbs
100ml milk
1 egg
4 tablespoons finely chopped herbs (a mixture of oregano, thyme and flat-leaf parsley)
Salt and freshly ground black pepper

One of the challenges when creating a cookbook is getting the balance right between great new ideas and old favourites. Everyone has had spaghetti and meatballs, but hopefully my ultra-simple recipe will inspire you to revisit this classic dish. In this recipe I bake the meatballs in the oven. I find it is just a little less faffy to cook them in one go like this rather than in a few batches in a frying pan, not least because you could find yourself with three or even four pans on the go, and that leads to two things: mess and lots of washing up.

I recommend making a double-sized batch of the tomato sauce and using the other half for the spicy sausage pasta bake on page 141.

1. First make the tomato sauce. Heat a good glug of olive oil in a saucepan over a medium heat and add the onion. Cook for 4 to 5 minutes, until soft, then add the garlic and cook for another couple of minutes. Chuck in the herbs, tomatoes, sugar (if using) and season well with salt and pepper. Add 100ml water and leave to simmer for 20 minutes.
2. Meanwhile, make the meatballs. Preheat the oven to 200°C/400°F/Gas Mark 6.
3. In a large bowl mix together all the meatball ingredients. Make sure you season it well with plenty of salt and pepper. A trick to check the seasoning is to fry a tiny piece of the mixture and see how it tastes.
4. Shape the mixture into small balls, about 2.5cm in diameter. Place them on a non-stick baking sheet (or a baking sheet lined with greaseproof paper) and cook for around 10 minutes, until the meatballs are hot all the way through and a little browned. When you put the meatballs in the oven, start cooking the pasta in a large pan of salted boiling water according to the packet instructions.

5. Just before serving, add the cooked meatballs to the simmering tomato sauce for a few minutes.
6. Serve the pasta with the sauce and meatballs spooned over the top, sprinkled with basil and freshly grated Parmesan.

Macaroni cauliflower cheese

Serves 2 adults and 2 children

You will need a 20 x 30cm baking dish

300g macaroni (or other pasta, if you prefer)

4 or 5 small cauliflower florets

1 small courgette, cut into cubes

30g butter, plus extra for greasing

30g plain flour

500ml milk

1 teaspoon Dijon mustard

A dash of Tabasco (optional)

75g grated extra-mature Cheddar cheese

½ teaspoon finely chopped thyme

Salt and freshly ground black pepper

2 tomatoes, deseeded and chopped

100g ham, cut into small cubes (optional)

For the topping

25g fresh breadcrumbs

1 tablespoon freshly grated Parmesan cheese

1 tablespoon grated mature Cheddar cheese

1 tablespoon finely chopped basil leaves

I ummed and aaahed about including a mac 'n' cheese recipe, but it fits this chapter so well and it is a staple in our house: two good reasons to include it! I have given it a little twist though by adding some vegetables, which cook in the pasta water, so there's no need for extra pans. You can pretty well use any vegetables you want here, but I have used a combination of cauliflower, courgette and tomatoes, turning it into a kind of macaroni cauliflower cheese! I also like to chuck some ham into this dish but you can, of course, leave it out if you want it to be vegetarian. Oh, and just to be controversial, you can use any other pasta shape too, although don't go calling this a macaroni cheese if you do!

1. Cook the macaroni in a large pan of salted boiling water according to the packet instructions. With 5 minutes left of its cooking time, add the vegetables and let them cook with the pasta. Drain and set aside.

2. Meanwhile, melt the butter in a saucepan on a medium heat. Add the flour and stir together for a couple of minutes, until well combined and the flour is cooked. You are looking for a nice golden brown colour. Gradually add the milk, whisking all the time, until you have a fairly thin white sauce.

3. Remove the sauce from the heat, mix in the mustard, Tabasco, cheese and thyme and stir well until the cheese is melted. Have a taste and season with salt and pepper if you think it needs it. Preheat your grill to its highest setting.

4. Grease a baking dish with butter and tip in the cooked pasta, vegetables, the chopped tomatoes and ham (if you're using it). Pour the sauce over the top and mix everything together.

5. Combine the topping ingredients and sprinkle them over the pasta. Place under the hot grill for about 10 minutes until golden brown. Serve immediately.

Chicken and olive pasta bake

I think I may be addicted to pasta. I would happily eat it several times a week. It has an instant ability to satisfy and soothe, while at the same time, being unbelievably quick and easy to prepare. That said, I am often happy to stretch the cooking time a little to make a pasta bake. The squelch of a big spoon scooping into a delicious bake has something so comforting about it. I'll admit that, on their own, capers are quite feisty but they add so much flavour and depth to all manner of dishes that I use them all the time without complaint from my discerning six- and three-year-old customers.

Serves 2 adults and 2 children

You will need a 20 x 30cm baking dish

350g penne or any other shape pasta

Olive oil

200g chicken thighs or breasts, skin removed and cut into small cubes

1 onion, finely chopped

2 garlic cloves, finely chopped

100ml white wine

2 tablespoons roughly chopped black olives

1 tablespoon capers, rinsed, drained and chopped

Zest of 1 lemon

1 teaspoon fennel seeds, crushed

200g soft cream cheese

Salt and freshly ground black pepper

2 tablespoons finely chopped flat-leaf parsley

50g freshly grated Parmesan cheese

100g grated Cheddar cheese

1. Cook the pasta in a large pan of salted boiling water according to the packet instructions.
2. Make sure it is al dente – you don't want it too soft yet, as it will cook a little more in the oven. Drain, reserving a mug of the cooking water.
3. About 10 minutes before the end of the pasta cooking time, heat some olive oil in a frying pan on a medium heat and add the chicken. Keep it moving around the pan until it is cooked on all sides.
4. Throw in the onion and cook for 3 to 4 minutes until softened, then stir in the garlic.
5. Turn up the heat and pour in the wine. Let it bubble up and then continue to cook for a couple of minutes to reduce. Preheat your oven to 180°C/350°F/Gas Mark 4.
6. Lower the heat and chuck in the olives, capers, lemon zest and fennel seeds.
7. Pour in the reserved pasta cooking water and spoon in the cream cheese. Stir well until the cheese is melted into the sauce. If it's a touch too thick, add a splash of water.
8. Season the sauce with salt and pepper, stir through the parsley and then mix in the pasta.
9. Plonk everything in a baking dish, cover with both the grated cheeses and bake for 20 to 25 minutes until golden on top and bubbling away nicely.

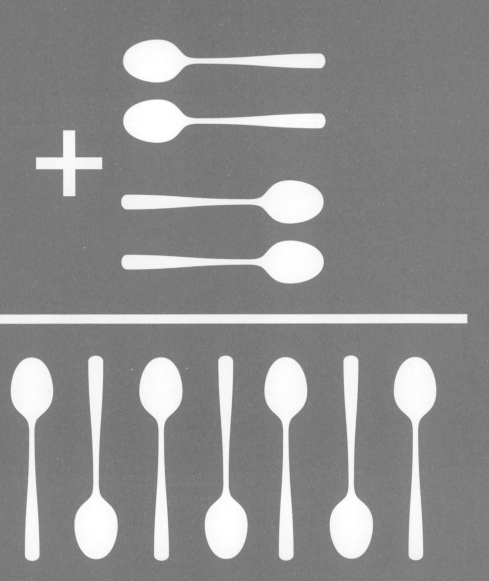

2+2=7

I think this chapter typifies the change in our mealtimes since Archie started school: what to do when, often at the last minute, you find yourself with an extended group of children to feed. Well, you turn to this chapter! Not only will they love eating all these dishes, they will also love how interactive they are. This is where food becomes part of the play date, a centrepiece of the afternoon or evening instead of an afterthought.

Bread and baked beans tartlets

Serves 4 children

You will need an 8-hole muffin tin

Butter

8 medium slices of bread, crusts removed

400g tin baked beans

2 large handfuls of grated Cheddar cheese

I cannot deny that this recipe is, of course, glorified beans on toast, but these tartlets are great fun to make together with children. They look impressive on the plate and can be as posh (or not) as you like. Try them with some fried bacon or sliced leftover sausages added to the beans. Tinned spaghetti works well here too, as does leftover pasta in a tomato sauce. And you can replace the Cheddar with mozzarella or Parmesan. Not only are these tartlets great to wheel out on play dates, but they are so versatile that they have become one of our fallback lunches – and are often eaten at breakfast time at the weekend too. Most importantly, these tartlets are a guaranteed mealtime success in my house, whenever they are served.

Preheat the oven to 180°C/350°F/Gas Mark 4.

1. Grease the muffin tin with butter and spread butter onto each slice of bread.
2. Push a slice of buttered bread gently into each muffin cup (buttered side on the tin), pressing it into the base and against the side. If you tear the bread, simply use a little bit from the corner of the slice to patch up the hole. Repeat with the rest of the bread.
3. Spoon the beans into the bread cups and top with grated cheese.
4. Bake in the oven for 20 to 25 minutes, until the bread is golden and crispy, the cheese has fully melted and the filling is piping hot. Serve immediately.

2+2=7

New York pancakes with bacon and syrup

These are the thicker, fluffier kind of pancakes. If they were big enough, you could have a very comfortable night's sleep on them. Unlike conventional French pancakes, they are dry fried, rather than in oil or butter. This also means that you avoid the perennial problem of the first pancake of the batch not working out properly. The original recipe for the batter comes from a lovely deli in Hitchin in Hertfordshire called Halsey's Deli which is now run by the colourful Damian, who was a Saville Row tailor in a previous life. For a play date, I serve these with crispy rashers of bacon, drizzled with syrup.

Makes approximately 18 pancakes

270 g plain flour

2 tsp baking powder

1 tsp salt

4 tbsp caster sugar

260 ml milk

2 large eggs

4 tbsp melted butter

10 rashers of bacon (smoked or unsmoked)

Golden Syrup or Maple Syrup (2 tbsp)

Vegetable or sunflower

1. First make your batter. Mix together the flour, baking powder, salt and caster sugar. Create a well in the middle and pour in the milk, egg and melted butter. Whisk, all the ingredients together, until you have a thick, gluey batter with no lumps.
2. Fry the bacon rashers in a large frying pan on a medium heat in a little drizzle of oil. When they are crispy, pour in the syrup to coat the bacon. Set the bacon to one side.
3. Heat a clean non-stick pan on a medium heat but don't put any oil into the pan. Dollop a tablespoon of the pancake batter into the pan, spreading it out a little with the back of your spoon. You want a round pancake of 3 inches in diameter.
4. Cook the pancakes up to 3 at a time for a couple of minutes until bubbles form on top, then flip them over and cook for a further minute until brown. Set these pancakes aside then repeat until all the batter is used up. This batter will give you around 18 pancakes. You can make the pancakes in advance and just warm them up for 20 seconds in the microwave or briefly in a frying pan on a low-medium heat.
5. Serve the bacon and pancakes in the middle of the table for the kids to tick into and share, not forgetting some extra syrup for drizzling.

2+2=7

DIY strawberry ice cream sundaes

Serves 4 children

You will need 4 tall glasses

Vanilla and/or strawberry
ice cream

A selection of fillings

Chocolate brownies or any
other kind of cake, broken
into pieces (leftovers work
perfectly)

Cookies or biscuits (the
peanut butter cookies on
page 171 are great in this)

A couple of meringue nests,
crumbled into pieces

Fresh fruit – strawberries,
bananas or pitted cherries
are especially good

For the caramel sauce

100g caster sugar

150g double cream

½ teaspoon vanilla extract

For the strawberry sauce

200g ripe strawberries

Sugar, to taste

A squeeze of lemon juice

My word, are DIY sundaes popular in my house?! Not
only are they (of course!) delicious, but they are fun to
put together too, especially if you have extra children
in the house. I also love the way I can use up the
broken ends of the biscuit packets I have lurking in the
cupboard – there really are no rules here as to what
goes in your sundae. Think of this more as a concept
than a single recipe. The caramel sauce is dead easy to
make, as is the strawberry sauce and both can be made
well in advance (keep them stored in the fridge and
reheat gently before using).

To make the caramel sauce

1. Put the sugar in a saucepan in an even layer. Heat it very
    slowly until it starts to melt around the edges. Now start
    swirling it gently, until all the sugar has melted and it has
    started to smoke and darken in colour.
2. Remove the pan from the heat and add half the
    cream, stirring quickly to make sure it is completely
    incorporated. Add the remaining cream and the vanilla
    extract and continue to stir. If you find you have clumps
    of hardened caramel, put the saucepan back over a very
    low heat and melt them back into the sauce.

2+2=7

To make the strawberry sauce

1. Hull the strawberries and blitz them in a blender. Add a tablespoon of sugar and give it a taste; add a little more sugar if you think it needs it. Add a squeeze of lemon and blitz again. If you want the sauce to be completely smooth, pass it through a sieve to remove the seeds.

To assemble the sundaes

1. Put everything on the table and let everyone add whatever they like to their sundae dishes. Word of advice: if you are using the squirty cream, keep a close eye on it. Cream 'gun' fights can break out ever so quickly . . . !

Toppings

Marshmallows, chopped nuts, crumbled Flakes, sprinkles

Whipped cream (or squirty cream)

2+2=7

Roast beef French dip

This recipe is a huge crowd pleaser. It successfully turns a fairly traditional joint of beef into a fun and interactive experience, thanks to the dipping gravy. I think it's an ideal dish to feed a group of hungry mouths on a play date, but it is just as effective as a family meal or as a twist on a classic Sunday roast. You can choose how well done you like your beef, but I like to cook mine medium-rare for this, in true French style. It has more flavour and the beef is lovely and tender. Cook it before you head off on the school run and then leave it to rest while you are out. Perfect.

Serves up to 8 children

1 small roasting joint of beef (approx. 750g–1kg)

Salt and freshly ground black pepper

2 teaspoons dried herbs (a mixture of oregano, rosemary and thyme works well)

Olive oil or beef dripping

2 onions, cut in half and finely sliced

1 tablespoon plain flour

100ml red wine

200ml beef stock

A good length of baguette for each person

Preheat the oven to 180°C/350°F/Gas Mark 4.

1. Season the meat with salt and pepper and sprinkle over the herbs. Heat the olive oil or dripping in a roasting dish on a medium to high heat on your hob.
2. Brown the meat well on all sides, then lay the onion slices in the base of the roasting dish and place the beef on top. Add a splash of water and roast the beef to your liking (a good guide is 20 minutes per 500g for rare, 25 minutes for medium-rare or 30 minutes for well done).
3. When cooked, remove the beef from the roasting dish. Cover it with foil and leave it to rest for half an hour.
4. To make the dipping gravy, put the roasting dish back on the hob on a medium heat, sprinkle in the flour and stir together thoroughly. Pour in the red wine and allow it to bubble for a few seconds while you use your spoon to scrape up any bits sticking to the bottom of the dish.
5. In goes the beef stock and simmer gently for 3 to 4 minutes until the gravy is slightly thickened and the onions are well cooked.
6. Remove the onions with a slotted spoon and keep to one side in a bowl. Pour any juices from the rested beef into the roasting dish then pour the whole lot into a wide jug.
7. Slice the beef thinly and serve it with the baguettes, onions and gravy at the table. Allow everyone to assemble a baguette and take it in turns to dip it in the gravy.

Vegetable fritters

These vegetable fritters are incredibly versatile and unbelievably delicious. You can use whatever vegetables you have to hand, plus your choice of cheese, which make them great fun to prepare with children as they can get involved in choosing the ingredients. Feta or Cheddar work very well but there's no need to limit yourself to just these two. The fritters are good served with slices of ham or chicken and go very nicely with some sweet chilli dipping sauce.

1. Whisk the egg whites until they reach the stiff peak stage (technically speaking, they should stay in the bowl if you hold it upside down over your head. You know you want to try this!).
2. Put the flour in a different bowl, pour in the milk and stir to combine. Don't worry: it will be very stiff to start with. Add the egg yolks and the spices and stir again.
3. Gently fold in the egg whites using a metal spoon.
4. Stir in your choice of vegetables and cheese. If you want, you can divide the batter and add different vegetables to each portion to create a variety of fritters.
5. Heat a really good glug of oil in a large frying pan on a medium heat. Drop tablespoonfuls of the fritter mixture into the oil and fry for 2 to 3 minutes on each side until golden brown and cooked in the middle.
6. Serve immediately, as these fritters are best eaten warm.

Serves 4 children

2 eggs, whites and yolks separated

100g plain flour

75ml milk

A pinch of paprika

A pinch of cayenne pepper

Salt and freshly ground black pepper

Your choice of fillings (you can use a combination, but don't use too much or the batter won't hold the filling together)

200g sweetcorn

200g frozen peas

1 courgette, grated

1 carrot, grated

Crumbled feta cheese

Grated hard cheese (Cheddar is great here)

Chopped fresh herbs (a mixture of mint, flat-leaf parsley and basil)

Vegetable oil or olive oil

2+2=7

Chocolate fondue

Serves 4–6 children

200g good-quality chocolate
1 teaspoon vanilla extract
200ml double cream

For dipping
Cubes of cake or brioche
Amaretti biscuits
Marshmallows
Chunks of fruit, such as
strawberries, cherries,
peaches, apricots, plums
or banana
Popping candy

I feel guilty that my sister and I endlessly took the mickey out of my mum for the burgundy-coloured fondue kit she bought and used once. I feel especially guilty because I love eating fondue with the children, especially when we have extra guests in the house. As with the sundaes on page 152, the possibilities here are endless. You can use any kind of chocolate that takes your fancy, although it's worth buying a good-quality chocolate, as it will have a better consistency when melted. Experiment with infusing the cream with different flavours, such as chilli, ginger, cinnamon, orange zest or fennel – simply warm the cream, remove it from the heat, add your chosen flavour and then let it cool down. Or, for an adult twist, mix in some instant espresso powder with a tiny bit of water, or even a teaspoon of rum! For extra fun, dip your fruits in popping candy after coating them in the chocolate. If you don't have a fondue set, both this and the butterscotch version on page 157 can be made without one (see the instructions within the method).

You'll also need wooden or metal skewers (or you can simply use forks)

1. If you have a fondue kit, simply break up the chocolate, put it in the fondue bowl with the vanilla extract and cream and melt it over a gentle heat.
2. If you don't have a fondue pot, put the ingredients in a heatproof bowl set over a saucepan of barely simmering water (don't let the bowl touch the water) and melt the ingredients together.
3. Give the sauce a good stir and serve while it is still warm, either in the fondue pot or in individual dishes or coffee cups, with the dipping ingredients in bowls on the table.

2+2=7

Butterscotch fondue

Butterscotch was made for dipping. Creamy and fudgey, fruit just loves being coated in it! It's the simplicity of this recipe that I really enjoy. Not only will the sauce be just as delicious poured over ice cream or served in a pancake, any leftovers can be kept in the fridge in an airtight container for a good few days. As with the chocolate fondue on page 156, you can make this even if you don't have a fondue kit (see the instructions within the method).

Serves 4–6 children

150g butter
150g dark brown sugar
200g double cream
1 teaspoon vanilla extract
A squeeze of lemon juice

For dipping

Chunks of fruit, such strawberries, cherries, peaches, apricots, plums or banana

You'll also need wooden or metal skewers (or you can simply use forks)

1. Simply cook all the ingredients in your fondue pot or in a saucepan on a low heat, stirring as you go. The sauce is ready when everything is fully melted together and your butterscotch is a lovely rich nutty fudge colour.
2. Leave the butterscotch to cool a little before serving it in the fondue pot or in individual bowls or coffee cups. Pile the fruit in the middle of the table and let everyone get dipping.

2+2=7

Cheese fondue

Serves 4–6 children

1 garlic clove, sliced
in half

200ml white wine

1 teaspoon lemon juice

275g grated Emmental
cheese

275g grated Gruyère
cheese

50g freshly grated
Parmesan or Cheddar
cheese

2 tablespoons brandy
(optional)

1 tablespoon cornflour

Salt and freshly ground
black pepper

A pinch of cayenne
pepper

For dipping

French bread (preferably
a little stale), cut into
cubes

Small new potatoes,
boiled or roasted

Cherry tomatoes

Chunks of Frankfurter
sausages

Button mushrooms

Cooked cauliflower and
broccoli florets

If you weren't given a fondue set when you got married (I'm sure it must appear in the top 20 most popular wedding gifts!), there are some very cheap models around, and I promise you, you will get loads of use out of it. They are perfect for hassle-free social occasions and, as such, they are ideal for this chapter. Gruyère, Emmental and Comté are the traditional cheeses used for a fondue but don't be afraid to experiment – you can even create an English-style fondue by using a combination of cheeses such as Red Leicester and mature Cheddar. For a completely English version, use cider or ale instead of the wine. If you want to make this entirely alcohol free, you can replace it with chicken stock but I think a little alcohol adds a lot of flavour and it also cuts through some of the richness of the cheese.

1. Rub the garlic all over the inside of the fondue bowl.
2. Pour in the white wine and lemon juice and heat over a low heat. Gradually add all the grated cheeses, stirring in a figure of eight, until completely melted.
3. If you're using the brandy, blend it with the cornflour; otherwise, mix the cornflour with a couple of tablespoons of water. Stir this into the fondue and cook for a further 2 to 3 minutes.
4. Season with salt, pepper and the cayenne pepper.
5. Put the fondue on the table, keeping a flame underneath. Give everyone a fondue fork and let them select their choice of food to dip.
6. Oh, and don't forget that one of the best bits is the toasted cheesy crust which forms on the bottom, called la réligieuse (which means 'nun'!). Pull it out and eat it when you're done!

2+2=7

Easy flatbread pizzas

Serves 4–6 children

For the flatbreads

250g strong white bread flour, plus extra for dusting

2 teaspoons dried instant yeast

1 teaspoon salt

1 teaspoon sugar

1 tablespoon plain yoghurt

4 tablespoons olive oil, plus extra for greasing

Traditional Turkish topping

1 onion, finely chopped

1 garlic clove, finely chopped

250g lamb mince

A good handful of chopped flat-leaf parsley

A pinch of ground cinnamon

A pinch of allspice

1 tomato, finely chopped

1 tablespoon tahini

2 tablespoons lemon juice or a pinch of sumac

2 tablespoons pine nuts

These flatbread pizzas are based on delicious, cheese-free Turkish Lahmacun. This makes them a particularly good option if you are following a diet without dairy. There is no cooking involved in the topping; it is just a case of mixing the ingredients in a bowl and spreading it over the bases! If you want to make these flatbread pizzas ultra quickly, use any of the flatbreads on sale in the supermarket. That said, if you do have a little extra time, the flatbread recipe is lovely to make yourself, or with your children. That would explain why these pizzas often get eaten in my house on a Sunday evening when, at a loose end towards the end of the day, getting Archie and Matilda involved in a bit of dough making is both fun and a great way of killing some tired time.

1. In a bowl, mix the flour with the yeast, salt and sugar.
2. Add the yoghurt, olive oil and 100ml water and use your hands to bring everything together to form a dough.
3. On a floured worktop, knead the dough lightly for about 5 minutes until it is nice and smooth (you can also use a dough hook in a food processor if you have one).
4. Lightly oil the bowl, put the dough back in, cover it in cling film and leave it to rise in a warm place for about an hour until it has doubled in size. This will take a little longer if it is a particularly cold day.
5. To make the topping, mix together all the ingredients (except the pine nuts). You can do this well in advance and refrigerate.
6. When you are ready to assemble the pizzas, preheat your oven as high as it will go. Heat a couple of upturned baking trays in the oven to cook the pizzas on.

2+2=7

7. Divide the dough into balls. You can make 4 large, 8 medium or 12 small pizzas from this amount. Give your worktop a good dusting of flour and roll out the flatbreads until they are nice and thin – but be careful not to tear them.

8. Spread some of the topping mixture over each flatbread and sprinkle with the pine nuts.

9. Dust the hot baking trays with flour, place the loaded flatbreads on top and cook them for 8 to 10 minutes – the breads will be cooked and a little crisp around the edge. Serve immediately. I like to put a medium flatbread on each baking tray, cook and serve them, and then cook the next batch while the first lot is being eaten at the table!

2+2=7

Tortilla wraps with home-made refried beans

Serves 4–6 children

I recommend using flour tortillas for this (allowing a couple per person) but tacos work too

For the meat filling

Olive oil

500g chicken meat (breast, leg or thigh), sliced

1 garlic clove

A pinch of ground cinnamon

A pinch of ground cloves

1 teaspoon cumin

½ teaspoon allspice

Salt and freshly ground black pepper

Chilli powder or chipotle paste, to taste (optional)

1 tablespoon tomato purée

This is a great social meal for children to enjoy on a play date or for a family to tuck into at the end of a trying day. I love the variety of textures and flavours and my children particularly enjoy having (almost!) complete control over what they are eating. Be prepared for things to get messy, but they will greatly enjoy filling their wraps and rolling them themselves. Refried beans are readily available in supermarkets but I really like making them myself, with the added benefit that I can control exactly how spicy (or not) I want them to be. Don't limit yourself to a meat filling; you can use mushrooms or firm-fleshed fish instead, cooked in the same way as the chicken. You can also use any kind of mince. I've included rice as one of the optional ingredients as this is a staple in a burrito, but don't try to pack in too much.

1. Heat a glug of olive oil in a frying pan. Add the chicken and cook over a high heat until it starts to brown.
2. Add the garlic, all the spices and seasonings and the tomato purée and stir to coat the chicken. Splash in a little water and simmer for a few minutes until the chicken is cooked through. Add more water if it looks like it's drying out.
3. To make the refried beans, use a masher or fork to mash the beans with a little water. You don't want them to be completely broken down; some texture is good and it's fine to leave a few whole.
4. Heat the butter or lard (or drizzle of oil) in a large frying pan. Cook the onion and garlic on a low heat until softened, add the coriander stems and chilli, and then stir in beans. Cook for a few minutes on a very low heat, stirring regularly so they don't stick to the pan. Add a touch more water if necessary. Season with salt and pepper and remove the pan from the heat.

2+2=7

5. Quickly make the tomato salsa by mixing together all the ingredients. Drizzle with olive oil.
6. Now you are ready to plonk everything on the table and let everyone assemble their wraps! Warm the tortillas in a dry frying pan or in the microwave and then enjoy the free-for-all as everyone chooses their combination of fillings. To create the perfect wrap, place the fillings in a line, about 5cm in from the edge of the tortilla. Fold over the top and bottom edges, then roll the tortilla over itself to create a tight wrap.

For the refried beans

400g tin beans, rinsed and drained (pinto beans or kidney beans work best here)

A large knob butter or lard (or vegetable oil)

1 onion, finely chopped

2 garlic cloves, finely chopped

1 tablespoon coriander stems

½ teaspoon chilli powder or chipotle paste, to taste

Salt and freshly ground black pepper

For the tomato salsa

6 medium tomatoes, deseeded and finely chopped

½ red onion, finely chopped

Juice of 1 lime

A pinch of brown sugar

A pinch of cumin

Salt and freshly ground black pepper

Olive oil

Your choice of fillings

Cooked white rice (for the full burrito experience)

Avocado, sliced and squeezed with lime juice

Sliced mango, squeezed with lime juice

Jalapeño peppers

Grated Cheddar cheese

Sour cream or crème fraîche

Fresh coriander leaves

Crisp lettuce (iceberg is good)

White cabbage, shredded

Grated carrot

2+2=7

Baked eggs

This simple play date idea works brilliantly when you have a crowd because the ramekins are so much fun to assemble. I would recommend offering a really good choice of fillings and just letting the children do their worst with them! I have found that by putting a dollop of double cream on top of each yolk, it will stay runny while it is baking. If you want a hard yolk, just leave off the cream. This is very much a pick-and-mix recipe, the only constant being the eggs themselves. Everything else is down to your personal taste.

You will need a ramekin for each egg

Butter

I recommend 2 large eggs per person

Salt and freshly ground black pepper

1 tablespoon double cream for each egg

1 tablespoon grated cheese for each egg (Cheddar or Gruyère work well)

Any combination of the following

Cubed ham

Chopped fried bacon

Fried chorizo or any other kind of sausage

Spinach, wilted in butter with a grating of nutmeg

Chopped fresh tomatoes

Sliced roasted red peppers

Tinned tuna or sardines, drained and mixed with a little mayonnaise

Mushrooms fried in butter with herbs and garlic

To serve

Toast soldiers

Blanched asparagus spears or sprouting broccoli florets

Raw courgette and carrot sticks

Oven-baked potato wedges

Preheat your oven to 180°C/350°F/Gas Mark 4.

1. Liberally butter each ramekin all around the inside and put a layer of your favourite combination of fillings in the bottom.
2. Carefully, break an egg on top and season it with some salt and pepper. Dollop a tablespoon of cream on top of the yolks if you want them soft set. Sprinkle over the cheese.
3. Place the ramekins on a baking tray and cook in the oven for exactly 12 minutes.
4. Take the ramekins out of the oven and leave them to cool down until they are safe to handle. Serve them at the table with all the dippy bits.

Absolutely instant chocolate mousse

A while back, I had the idea of using yoghurt in a chocolate mousse, thinking it would make a lighter mousse compared with the traditional method that uses egg yolks. I actually discovered that the addition of the yoghurt makes the mousse set almost instantly! No need for it to chill in the fridge, it is ready to eat as soon as you've finished mixing. As such, it's ideal for impromptu play dates – or any last minute event for that matter. The only downside with this recipe is that as the pay-off for the mousse setting so quickly, the egg yolks are wasted, but you could always keep them fresh in the fridge and use them to enrich an omelette.

Serves 4 children

200g good-quality
dark chocolate

4 egg whites

4 tablespoons caster sugar

140g Greek yoghurt
(0% if possible – I like Total)

Mini marshmallows, to serve

1. Melt the chocolate in a heatproof bowl set over a saucepan of gently simmering water (make sure the bowl doesn't actually touch the water) or in the microwave for 2 minutes, stirring well halfway through. Allow the melted chocolate to cool a little.
2. Whisk the egg whites until they form stiff peaks, then carefully whisk in the sugar, a little at a time.
3. Mix the yoghurt into the cooled chocolate. You will see it starting to thicken already.
4. Using a metal spoon, fold about one-quarter of the whisked egg whites into the chocolate, just to loosen it up a little. Fold in the eggs by moving the spoon in a figure of eight, while at the same time slowly turning the bowl.
5. Gently fold in the rest of the eggs, taking care not to beat the air out of them.
6. Spoon the mousse into bowls, mugs or ramekins and serve immediately with the mini marshmallows scattered on top.

2+2=7

Genius Treats

This is a chapter to put a smile on the faces of adults and children alike, and I had so much fun creating the recipes. I think that cakes, sweets and treats are an important part of my children's diet. Let's face it: there are some mealtimes when a good bit of home-made cake is all that will end up being eaten. I am not the world's most precise baker, which is reflected in this collection of foolproof desserts.

Blocko's blooming brilliant chocolate marshmallow fudge cake

Yes, you read that correctly! Chocolate. Marshmallow. Fudge. Need I say more?! Paul Bloxham is an extremely fine chef. Quality pub grub is his speciality, but he is also a dad to three young children so he knows all about the importance of giving them great food, cooked simply. This is his recipe and he has kindly given me permission to use it. It is quite simply a stunner. A show-stopper for your children and their friends to enjoy. It's best to make this for a group of people, as it does not last well once it has cooled; it loses moisture and you will miss out on all its lovely chocolate-y gooeyness.

Preheat your oven to 180°C/350°F/Gas Mark 4.

1. Line the cake tin with greaseproof paper.
2. Melt your butter gently in a small saucepan or in the microwave and leave it to cool for a few minutes.
3. Sift the flour, half of the cocoa powder, the baking powder and the salt into a large bowl.
4. In a separate bowl, whisk together the eggs, caster sugar, melted butter, milk and vanilla extract.
5. Add the wet mixture to the dry mixture and stir the batter until just combined.
6. Mix in the walnuts and marshmallows and tip the batter into the prepared tin. Smooth the surface to create an even layer.

Makes 10 slices

You will need a 20cm square cake tin
200g unsalted butter
225g plain flour
175g unsweetened cocoa powder
¾ teaspoon baking powder
¾ teaspoon salt
2 large eggs
200g caster sugar
150ml milk
1 teaspoon vanilla extract
125g chopped walnuts
150g marshmallows

For the topping
100g dark chocolate
200g Demerara sugar
225ml boiling water
Crème fraîche or ice cream, to serve

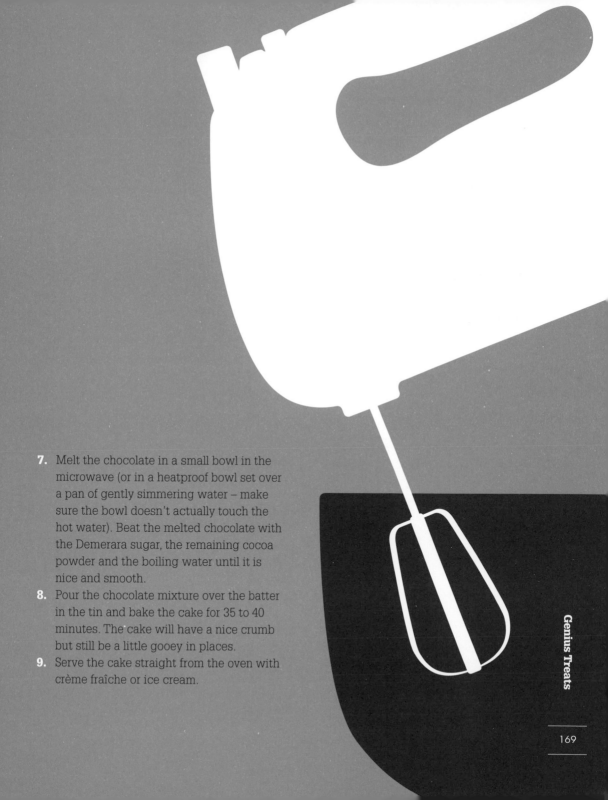

7. Melt the chocolate in a small bowl in the microwave (or in a heatproof bowl set over a pan of gently simmering water – make sure the bowl doesn't actually touch the hot water). Beat the melted chocolate with the Demerara sugar, the remaining cocoa powder and the boiling water until it is nice and smooth.

8. Pour the chocolate mixture over the batter in the tin and bake the cake for 35 to 40 minutes. The cake will have a nice crumb but still be a little gooey in places.

9. Serve the cake straight from the oven with crème fraîche or ice cream.

Genius Treats

Apple and cinnamon tray bake

Tray bakes are lifesavers for clumsy bakers like me. They require less attention than cakes and are generally more forgiving. This tray bake uses a classic combination of flavours and the simple addition of a crumble topping gives it a lovely extra crunch. If you want to make the method even more simple and quick, just blitz all of the main tray bake ingredients (except the apples) in your food processor.

Makes 16 pieces

You will need a deep 20 x 30cm baking tray

300g plain flour

2 teaspoons baking powder

1 teaspoon ground cinnamon

1 teaspoon mixed spice

150g butter

250g light soft brown sugar

4 eggs

250ml buttermilk

2 eating apples, peeled, cored and chopped

2 tablespoons Demerara sugar

For the crumble topping

50g butter, broken into lumps

80g plain flour

30g Demerara sugar

1 teaspoon ground cinnamon

Preheat the oven to 180°C/350°F/Gas Mark 4.

1. Line the baking tray with greaseproof paper.
2. Sift together the flour, baking powder and spices into a bowl.
3. In a separate, larger bowl, cream together the butter and light brown sugar until fluffy.
4. Add the eggs one at a time to the butter and sugar, alternating with heaped tablespoons of the flour mixture and the buttermilk, until everything is incorporated.
5. Toss the apple pieces in the Demerara sugar and scatter them over the batter. Scrape everything into the prepared tin.
6. To make the simple crumble topping, rub the butter into the flour until it forms crumbs, then stir in the Demerara sugar and cinnamon. Sprinkle over the batter and apples.
7. Bake for 45 to 55 minutes, until the cake is firm and starting to shrink away from the sides of the tin.
8. This cake can be served warm or cold.

Peanut butter cookies

These are proper soft and chewy American-style cookies. Despite their name, these cookies don't taste overly 'peanutty', so they probably won't offend anyone who doesn't normally enjoy peanut butter. The actual cookie recipe is a great base for adding other ingredients. I like to mix in a really good handful of chocolate chips for extra flavour and texture.

Makes about 16

110g butter at room temperature, broken into small lumps

100g soft light brown sugar

100g caster sugar

125g crunchy peanut butter

1 teaspoon vanilla extract

1 egg

200g plain flour, plus extra to dust

½ teaspoon baking powder

¼ teaspoon bicarbonate of soda

50g crushed peanuts

Preheat the oven to 180°C/350°F/Gas Mark 4.

1. Line 2 large baking trays with greaseproof paper.
2. Using an electric hand whisk on a low speed or a wooden spoon beat the butter in a large bowl until soft. Add the sugars and then beat together, until very light and fluffy.
3. Continue beating, adding in the peanut butter, vanilla extract and egg until nicely combined.
4. In a separate bowl, sift together the flour with the baking powder and bicarbonate of soda. Add this to the mix, along with the peanuts.
5. On a lightly floured worktop, use a rolling pin to shape small handfuls of the dough into round cookies, about 5cm in diameter and 2cm high.
6. Place the cookies on the prepared baking trays, leaving about 10cm between each one, as they will spread out as they cook. Press down each cookie with the back of a fork.
7. Bake for about 10 minutes until the cookies are set around the edges but still a little soft in the middle. Remove them from the oven and leave them on their baking trays for 5 minutes, where they will continue to cook. Finally, transfer them to a wire cooling rack.

Genius Treats

Fizzy lemon and popping candy cake

Makes 8 slices

You will need 2 x 20cm round sandwich tins

225g butter, at room temperature

225g caster sugar

Zest and juice of 2 lemons

4 eggs

225g self-raising flour

A good handful of popping candy (now available in the baking section of supermarkets)

For the filling

150–200g lemon curd, at room temperature

For the icing

300g cream cheese

Zest and juice of 1 lemon

50g icing sugar

2–3 tsp sherbet (from a Dip Dab or Sherbet Fountain)

This is a really fun cake! To this day, the look of bewilderment combined with joy on Archie's face when he first tasted popping candy remains one of my most enduring memories from when he was a toddler. Everyone loves a lemon drizzle cake, and this one is turbo-charged with a big smile! The sherbet does make this a rather sweet cake, but it adds a lovely fizz to the icing, and your children will love it.

Preheat the oven to 180ºC/350˚F/Gas Mark 4.

1. Line the sandwich tins with greaseproof paper.
2. Cream together the butter and sugar with the lemon zest in a large bowl, until light and fluffy.
3. Add the eggs, one at a time, with alternate spoonfuls of flour. Then fold in the remaining flour. (Alternatively, blitz together the butter, sugar, zest, flour and eggs in a food processor until smooth.)
4. Add the lemon juice, a little at a time, until you have a good dropping consistency (you don't want it to be runny, so you may not need it all).
5. Scrape the mixture into the prepared tins. Bake for 20 to 25 minutes, until golden brown and just starting to come away from the edges of the tins. Leave to cool in the tins for a few minutes then turn out onto wire cooling racks.
6. While the cakes are cooling, make the icing. First, beat the cream cheese until very soft and then add the lemon zest and juice, the icing sugar and sherbet. Continue to beat until it is light and airy.
7. To assemble, spread one of the cakes with a fairly thin layer of the icing, then swirl through the lemon curd. Sprinkle over a couple of good pinches of the popping candy.

8. Place the other cake on top and spread with the rest of the icing. You can also cover the side of the cake, if you like; you'll just need to spread the icing a little more thinly.

9. Decorate the surface with the rest of the popping candy just before serving. You can either sprinkle it all over the cake or, for a pretty effect, cut out a small star from the middle of a piece of paper and use the paper as a stencil to create little stars packed with popping candy.

Classic jammy dodgers

Give me a jammy dodger and I'm thrown straight back to my childhood, hanging out with my grandparents. The beauty of making your own is that you can vary the shape of your biscuits and also use whatever flavoured jam you fancy. In an ideal world, you will use a small cutter, around 1.5cm in diameter, to remove the hole in the top biscuit but, if you don't have one, you can use the point of a sharp knife to cut out a small opening yourself. Being a hit across the generations, these biscuits are also lovely to give as gifts.

Makes 8–10

250g butter, at room temperature

100g caster sugar

Zest of 1 lemon (optional)

350g plain flour, plus extra for dusting

1 egg yolk

1 teaspoon vanilla extract

150g jam of your choice (it should be smooth and not too runny)

Icing sugar, to dust (optional)

1. Using an electric hand whisk or a wooden spoon cream together the butter, sugar and optional lemon zest in a large bowl. Sift in the flour, then add the egg yolk and using your hands bring the dough together to form a ball. Alternatively, you can just whizz all the above ingredients together in a food processor. Wrap the dough in cling film and chill it in the fridge for 30 minutes.
2. Preheat your oven to 140°C/275°F/Gas Mark 1 and line a couple of baking trays with greaseproof paper.
3. Generously flour your work surface, divide the dough in half and knead the balls just a little to make the dough more pliable. Dust your rolling pin with flour, too, and then roll out both pieces of dough to a thickness of about 3mm.
4. Cut out as many biscuits as you can, using a cutter of any shape that is roughly 6cm wide. Cut a small hole (1.5cm) in the middle of half of your biscuits.
5. Arrange the biscuits on the lined baking trays (leaving a good gap between them, as they will spread a little as they cook) and bake for 20 to 30 minutes, until they start turning golden brown round the edges.
6. Remove from the oven and leave to cool on a wire rack.
7. When they have cooled, spread a good layer of jam on to the biscuits without a hole, then top each one with a biscuit with a hole. You want the jam to spread to the edges inside the biscuit. Top up the hole with extra jam then dust with icing sugar, if you like.
8. Your jammy dodgers should keep for at least a week in an airtight container.

Strawberry and apple leather strips

These are a marvellous way of impressing your children and making them believe that you are a genius confectioner. Willy Wonka would have been proud of these. They are like the chewy fruity strips you can buy for babies who are weaning, or the kind of Catherine Wheel sweets you find in pick-and-mix boxes. And yet, they are made from only fresh fruit, honey and lemon, with not a nasty ingredient in sight. I would even be as bold as to say that a strip of this leather could possibly constitute one of your five a day. Healthy and guilt-free snacking. You can use any combination of fruit here, as long as you stick to proportions of 150g of honey to every kilo of fruit.

Depends on the size!

500g strawberries, hulled
500g cooking apples, peeled, cored, chopped
Juice of 1 lemon
150g honey

Preheat your oven to its lowest setting (we're talking 50°C/120°F/Gas Mark 1/8 here).

1. Put the fruit in a saucepan with a splash of water and the lemon juice. Heat it gently, until the fruit is very soft.
2. Stir in the honey, then push the mixture through a sieve to remove all the bits.
3. Line a couple of baking trays with greaseproof paper. Divide the fruit pulp between the trays, using a spatula to spread it out as evenly as you can. You want a thickness of about 5mm.
4. Put the baking trays in the oven and leave them until the leather has dried out. You still want the leather to be very slightly tacky, as you are going to roll it. This will take between 10 to 12 hours, so is best done overnight.
5. Peel the leather away from the greaseproof paper, cut it into long 2cm-wide slices and then roll the slices into wheels (my children love doing this part).
6. And here's the best part of this recipe: these fruity leathers will keep for several months. Just store them in layers (separated by greaseproof paper) in an airtight container.

Plum and almond crumble

Serves 6

You will need a deep, 20 x 20cm baking dish

750g plums, halved and stones removed

3–4 tablespoons caster sugar, depending on the sweetness of the plums

For the crumble topping

150g chilled butter, broken into small lumps

250g spelt flour

100g soft light brown sugar

50g flaked almonds

Hand on heart, I have yet to meet a child who doesn't like a good crumble. There's just something unbelievably delicious about a melting buttery topping and slightly sweetened fruit. As a bonus, this is a bit healthier than the traditional version, as it uses spelt flour, which is readily available in supermarkets. It gives the crumble a slightly rougher texture and a bit of a nutty taste, which I really like, but if you prefer, you can just use regular plain flour. To make this gluten free, just swap the flour for gluten-free flour.

Preheat your oven to 190°C/375°F/Gas Mark 5.

1. Butter your baking dish, arrange the plums in the bottom (cut-side up) and then sprinkle with the sugar.
2. Bake in the oven for 15 minutes. Cooking them in the oven first, rather than in a saucepan, will stop the plums collapsing and will ensure that they will be perfectly cooked through when the crumble is baked.
3. Rub the butter into the spelt flour using your fingers until you have a lovely crumbly mixture. Stir in the brown sugar and the almonds.
4. Tip the crumble mix on top of the cooked plums, spreading it out nice and evenly, but without pressing down too much.
5. Bake the crumble for 25 minutes until the crumble topping is golden brown.
6. You can serve this crumble warm (with some cream or ice cream) or leave it to cool down completely and eat it cold.

Egg-free malted chocolate ice cream

Ice cream recipes often ask for egg yolks but this comforting, malty, chocolate ice cream is completely egg–free. This has two benefits. First, it means it is suitable for anyone who is allergic to eggs. Secondly, it means that you can use it as a milkshake instead by simply half-freezing the mixture! I've used milk chocolate here but there's no reason why you can't use dark chocolate or even white chocolate, if you prefer. Whichever you choose, it really is worth buying a good-quality chocolate, as you will notice the different in the final product. Although having an ice cream maker will speed up the whole process, it's not difficult to make this ice cream without one.

Serves 6–8

500ml double cream

50g cocoa powder

200g caster sugar

1 tablespoon malt extract (optional)

150g good-quality milk chocolate

200ml milk

4 tablespoons Horlicks malted drink powder

A packet of crushed and crumbled Maltesers, to serve

Preheat the oven to 180°C/350°F/Gas Mark 4.

1. Put the cream, cocoa powder, sugar and malt extract (if using) in a saucepan. Whisk them together thoroughly and then heat gently on a low heat until the sugar and malt extract have dissolved. Turn up the heat, bring to the boil and then immediately remove the pan from heat.
2. Break up the chocolate and add it to the cream, stirring it gently to melt it through the mixture.
3. Whisk the Horlicks powder into the milk and then add this to the rest of the ingredients and combine well.
4. If you have an ice cream maker, simply cool the creamy chocolate a little, then churn it in the ice cream maker and keep it in your freezer. If you don't have an ice cream maker, pour the mix into a large, shallow container (with a lid) and put it in the freezer. Whisk very thoroughly every 30 minutes until it is completely frozen. This ensures plenty of air gets in giving you a lovely smooth ice cream.
5. Serve with the crumbled Maltesers sprinkled on top.

Summer fruit jellies

Making jelly at home is absolutely child's play! As with so many recipes in this book, you'll get all the goodness of a traditional treat, without any of the E numbers or additives you would rather avoid. You can use any juice that takes your fancy or, for an extra bit of fun, why not create two different coloured jellies and allow one to set on top of the other in the glasses? As with your choice of juice, play around with what fresh fruit you use too. It's hard to think of any fruits that I wouldn't recommend, although I don't think the texture of banana would work as well in this jelly.

Serves 4

You'll need 4 medium-sized glasses

5 leaves of gelatine

500ml fruit juice of your choice (I think smooth works slightly better)

Juice of ½ a lime

About 2 tablespoons honey

A couple of good handfuls of freshly chopped fruit

1. Break up the gelatine leaves and put them in a small bowl. Pour just a little of your fruit juice over the top and then leave the leaves to soften for a few minutes.
2. Put the rest of the juice in a saucepan with the lime juice and honey and heat through on a low heat until the honey dissolves.
3. Keeping the juice on a gentle heat, add the gelatine and the soaking liquid and stir until everything is combined. Be careful not to boil the liquid.
4. Divide the fresh fruit between the serving glasses and fill each glass about one-third of the way up with the jelly liquid.
5. Put the glasses in the fridge and wait for the jelly to start to set. (Setting it in layers like this is the best way of ensuring that all the fruit doesn't float to the top of your glasses.) If you are tight for time, you can speed up this part of the process by putting the glasses in the freezer.
6. Once the jelly is firming up, divide the rest of the jelly liquid between the four glasses and put them back in the fridge to fully set. This can take 4 to 6 hours.

White chocolate and blueberry blondies

Gooey, cakey and extremely moreish, these blondies are made in a different way from a lot of blondie recipes, as the white chocolate is not melted down as part of the batter but is instead mixed through before baking. This means that they keep their strong butterscotch flavour. Having been known to eat these just before bed, I can confirm that they are perfect at all times of the day.

Preheat the oven to 180°C/350°F/Gas Mark 4.

1. Line your baking tray with greaseproof paper or oiled foil.
2. Melt the butter gently in a small saucepan over a low heat, or in a dish in the microwave. Allow it to cool a little, then mix it with the sugar in a large bowl until nicely combined. Add the eggs and vanilla extract.
3. In a separate bowl, mix the flour and baking powder together and fold this into the wet ingredients.
4. Stir in the chocolate chips and then scrape the batter into the prepared tin.
5. Sprinkle over the blueberries and bake in the oven for 25 to 30 minutes until firm and the top has started to crack. The blondies need to cool completely before being cut up and served.

Makes 16 pieces

You will need a deep
20 x 30cm baking tray

175g butter

300g soft light brown sugar

2 large eggs

1 teaspoon vanilla extract

225g plain flour

1 teaspoon baking powder

100g white chocolate chips
(or put a 100g block of white chocolate in a sandwich bag and crush it into small chips using a rolling pin)

150g blueberries

Watermelon slush

Serves 4

Approx. 900g cubed, deseeded watermelon (this is about one-quarter of a large melon or half of a small one)

150–200g strawberries, hulled

Juice of 1 lime

1 tablespoon honey

A cheekily simple and extremely refreshing summer slush drink. And if you want to be extra cheeky, adults can add a shot of tequila and turn it into a frozen Margarita! Make sure you keep an eye on who has which glass though! For extra speed, buy a seedless watermelon, otherwise you'll need to spend a few minutes cutting around the seeds and then deseeding the rest. Double up the quantities and keep an extra batch in the freezer, then simply allow the slush to defrost a little just before serving. (If you have any leftover watermelon, try making the salad on page 112.)

Mint is a lovely addition to these flavours, but it can make the slush have a rather bitty texture. If you want to use some, melt the honey with 50ml water, add lots of fresh or dried mint and leave it to infuse for 15 minutes. Strain the leaves and add the minty syrup to the watermelon when blitzing.

1. Freeze the watermelon pieces in a covered container for at least 2 hours.
2. Blitz the frozen watermelon with the remaining ingredients in a food processor or blender.
3. If you want the slush to be slightly diluted, add some extra ice while you blitz it.
4. Serve immediately.

Lime and mango cheesecake pots

These little cheesecake pots are ideal to make in advance because they freeze really well. Leave them at room temperature while you eat your main course and they will be the perfect consistency just in time for dessert! This recipe makes 10 to 12 cupcake-sized pots. You can buy glass ramekins very cheaply, or you can just as easily use a muffin tin lined with paper cupcake cases. If the pots have been frozen, your kids will have loads of fun ripping away the wrapper and eating them with their fingers. There are a couple of important things to note here: first, please use proper cream. If you use one of the cream alternatives, the mixture is likely to split when you add the lime. Secondly, don't over-beat the cream, as that could also cause it to split when you mix everything together.

1. Melt the butter in the microwave (it only needs a minute or so) or in a saucepan on a low heat.
2. Put the biscuits in a sandwich bag and bash them with a rolling pin to turn them into crumbs.
3. Mix the biscuits into the butter and divide the mixture between the ramekins or muffin cases. Press down well to get a nice firm base.
4. Beat together the cream cheese, sugar and double cream. Add the zest and juice of the limes and beat again, then gently fold through the mango pieces. Spoon this on top of the biscuit bases.
5. You could do worse than serve these pots immediately, although the cream mixture will not have firmed up. Ideally, leave them to chill in the fridge for a couple of hours or bung them in the freezer for 20 to 30 minutes to firm up.
6. If you are feeling creative, decorate with fine curls of lime zest before serving.

Makes 10–12 small pots

You will need 10 to 12 ramekins or muffin cases

75g butter

150g biscuits (digestives or ginger nuts are ideal)

300g cream cheese (I like Philadelphia)

75g caster sugar

100ml double cream

Zest and juice of 2 limes

1 mango, peeled and cut into small cubes

Long curls of lime zest, to decorate (optional)

Luxury gluten-free chocolate brownies

Makes 16 pieces

You will need a deep
20 x 30cm baking tray

100g unsalted butter

200g good-quality dark chocolate (minimum 70 per cent cocoa solids, and make sure it is gluten free)

4 large eggs

250g caster sugar (preferably golden caster sugar)

100g ground almonds

100g chopped walnuts (optional)

Slightly crunchy on the outside but still soft and deliciously gooey in the middle . . . it's not difficult to achieve pure brownie perfection; you just have to make sure you don't overcook them. The best brownie I have eaten recently was made by a chef who is local to me, called Hendrik Dutson Seinfeld. As is so often the case with great chefs, he was more than happy to share his recipe and I have since adapted it to produce this wonderful flourless, gluten-free version.

Preheat your oven to 180°C/350°F/Gas Mark 4.

1. Line your baking tray with greaseproof paper or oiled foil.
2. Gently melt the butter and chocolate together, either in a dish in the microwave, or in a heatproof bowl set over a pan of gently simmering water (don't let the bowl actually touch the hot water). Allow it to cool a little once melted.
3. Meanwhile, in a large bowl, whisk together the eggs and sugar for a minute or two. You are looking for the sugar to be fully incorporated into the eggs and for the mixture to take in a little air, but don't over-whisk.
4. Pour the melted chocolate and butter into the eggs and sugar and stir well.
5. Add the ground almonds, together with the walnuts if you are using them. Fold them through the batter until you have a smooth and even mixture.
6. Scrape the mixture into your prepared tin and bake in the oven. Check on it after 20 minutes and if the top has already risen and is starting to crack a little, you can remove it from the oven. If the surface still looks a little raw in the middle, cook for a further 5 minutes and then check again.

7. Leave it to cool in the tin (the inside will carry on cooking a little) then cut into brownie-sized chunks.
8. The brownies will taste even better the following day and can be kept for 2 or 3 days in an airtight container. However, the likelihood is they will be gone by morning.

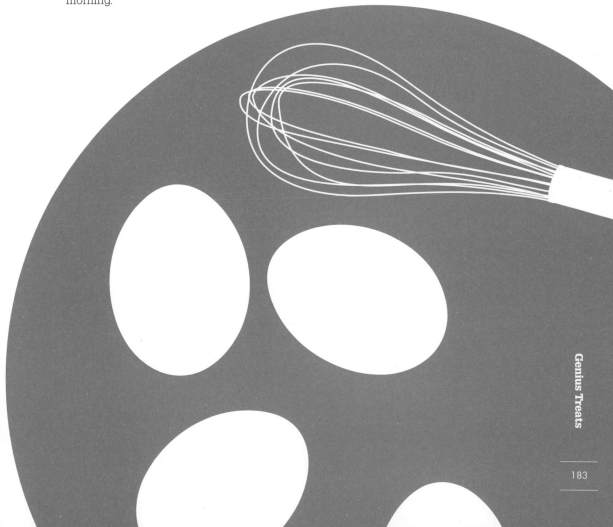

Home-made honeycomb chocolates

Vegetable or sunflower oil

8 tablespoons caster sugar

4 tablespoons golden syrup

1 level teaspoon bicarbonate of soda

200g good-quality dark chocolate

You will need a deep 20 x 20cm baking tray and a good deep saucepan

Archie and I spent a great Saturday morning hanging out together in the kitchen developing these wonderful Crunchie, sorry, crunchy sweet treats. We have since made a slightly odd discovery and so I feel I should give you a small warning about climactic conditions! It would appear that if you make honeycomb on a very hot or very damp and humid day, your chances of success are significantly reduced. I am unsure of the science behind this but it leads me to conclude that autumn and winter are the best seasons for making honeycomb.

1. Line your baking tray with greaseproof paper and then lightly oil the paper with vegetable or sunflower oil (honeycomb is very sticky stuff and it won't leave your paper alone if it can get away with it).
2. Put your deep saucepan on a medium heat. Pour in the sugar and golden syrup and heat, stirring gently, making sure all the sugar dissolves. As soon as the sugar has dissolved, stop stirring. Immediately!
3. Turn down the heat to low and let the syrup bubble and simmer very gently for 5 minutes. You definitely do not want a fierce bubble here, and do not stir it. Let it slowly turn into a caramel. You are going to have to trust your nose and eyes – don't let it smell of burning and make sure it isn't turning too dark. Once or twice, you can ever so slightly fold the mixture with your spatula, to make sure it stays an even colour (but don't overdo it or you will affect the temperature of the syrup – and don't scrape around the edges).

4. When the caramel has reached a nutty brown colour (not too dark; not too light), take the pan off the heat and dust in the level teaspoon of bicarbonate of soda. Fold it in immediately using a whisk but, again, don't overwork it.
5. Now leave it to bubble and rise up inside the saucepan like a volcano (your children will love watching this but remember we are dealing with scalding hot syrup, so this really is for an adult to do).
6. Once it has stopped rising, pour it into the prepared dish. Don't scoop out any of the honeycomb mix that doesn't naturally fall out of the pan. Anything you scoop will have the air knocked out of it and will turn to toffee. At this stage, rush the pan to the sink and fill it with very hot water. If you don't, you will be getting the hammer and chisel out later to get the honeycomb off the inside of your pan!
7. Leave the honeycomb to set. This will take 20 to 30 minutes. When it is set, break it up into bite-sized pieces.
8. Melt the chocolate in the microwave or in a small heatproof bowl set over a pan of gently simmering water (don't let the bowl actually touch the hot water).
9. Using your fingers or a skewer, dip the honeycomb pieces into the melted chocolate and then place them on greaseproof paper to set. The chocolate ensures the honeycomb stays fresh, so make sure you fully cover each piece.

Yoghurt and lemon curd crème brûlée

These crème brûlées don't actually involve any cooking, apart from the heat required to give them a crunchy topping. Putting them together is simply a case of mixing the ingredients – the thick Greek yoghurt gives them all the texture they need and the tangy flavour comes from the lemon curd. Don't worry if you don't have a blowtorch in your kitchen, if you grill them under a high heat you will get a more than acceptable finish.

Serves 4

You will need 4 x 150–200ml ramekins (7–8cm wide)

300ml Greek yoghurt

100ml half-fat crème fraîche

1 tablespoon honey

4 tablespoons lemon curd (or any flavour you fancy)

4 tablespoons blueberries

4 tablespoons granulated sugar (not caster)

If you are using your grill, preheat it to its very highest setting.

1. Whisk together the yoghurt, crème fraîche and honey until you have a smooth mixture and all the honey is well incorporated.
2. Put a tablespoon of curd in the bottom of each ramekin and top with a tablespoon of blueberries.
3. Divide the yoghurt mixture between the ramekins and sprinkle over the sugar. You want a good, even layer of sugar, covering all the creamy mixture.
4. Either brown the sugar with a blowtorch or place the ramekins on a baking tray and cook them under the very hot grill until the sugar has melted, turned a rich brown and is bubbling away. Under no circumstances touch the melted sugar while it is hot, as it will seriously burn you.
5. Allow the sugar to cool and then chill the brûlées in the fridge before serving. They will have a lovely crisp topping.

Index

Acknowledgements

A huge thank you to everyone who continues to follow my blog and follow me elsewhere, such as on my radio show. Thank you also to everyone who bought the first book – I hope you enjoy this one too. None of this would happen without your brilliant support.

Thank you to my superb team at Hodder & Stoughton – Sarah Hammond, Nicky Ross, Emma Knight and everyone else involved in the various stages on this book – for all their patience and creativity. And more patience.

Catherine Phipps' help, advice and friendship during the recipe development process was invaluable.

Thank you to my two brilliant agents for all their hard work and support – Clare Hulton for my books and Richard Howells at Somethin' Else for all his work on the other aspects of my career.

To all my friends and colleagues at BBC Three Counties Radio, thank you for everything you do which makes being on the radio such a constant pleasure for me.

I am totally indebted to everyone who gave up their time to test my recipes. Their help was priceless: Jenny Boler, Eimear Carvill, Karen Chaplin, Jo Cloke, Lisa Conley, Clare Cuckow, Alison and Graham Dear, Stew Denholm, Nicky Desmond, Miff Dunn, Lyse Edwards, Christine Evans, Rosie Fean, Emma Ferns, Lisa Glanville, Simon Glazier, Karen Goodwin, Michelle Groom, Nicola Guy, Penelope Hankey, Rachel Hartell, Denise Hayes, Judith Hayton, Maddy Hill, Aisling Holmes, Sarah and Jack Holmes, Laura Hoskison, Andy Hurry, Sylvia James, Katie Jansen, Sal Jefford, Kate Jones, Janice Kirkwood, Emily Lamboy, Rachel Locke, David Millar, Clare Morgan, Jennie Moore, Kate Notarianni, Wendy Orr, Cassie Pearse, Anthony Pike, Fiona Preece, Martina Rafter, Clair Rankin, Heidi Roberts, Helen Robinson, Claire Slim, Rachel Suddrick, Anna Story, Louise Teal, Ian Thake, Meg Thomas, Liz Tumner, Lisa Wakefield, Lisa Willes, Sian Williams, Elizabeth Wright, Kate York, Snow Yule.

To my friends and family, thank you for all your love, support, encouragement and patience over the last few years, without which I would be very lost. Thank you Jo for keeping me sane and for being there come what may, and to my parents, sister and in-laws for all their guidance and help and their ability to just drop anything to help us when we need them.

And finally, Archie and his willing sous-chef Matilda. You both have the priceless ability to keep me on my toes, to brighten my days, to keep me grounded and to just make me smile and laugh. I am so proud watching you both grow into your very individual personalities and love you both more than you can know.